PRAISE FOR *THE ART OF COORIE*

"Like a good malt whisky, *The Art of Coorie* shines Scotland in a lovely warm glow."
Kirsty Wark, presenter of BBC's *Newsnight*

"I was completely charmed by *The Art of Coorie*. It is a fine word indeed and a deeply pleasing notion. Gabriella's musings and discoveries are timely. All of my associations with coorie come from childhood – being invited to feel welcome, safe and loved, close by the side of someone making just enough room. It's high time the concept of coorie was more widely known. We've long valued the thought here in Scotland and now it can go out to the wider world and wrap up more folk, make them warm and well. Coorie is good for the heart and the soul."
Neil Oliver, presenter of BBC's *Coast* and author of *A History of Scotland*

"*The Art of Coorie* is a wonderful celebration of contemporary Caledonian cool."
Geoff Allan, author of *The Scottish Bothy Bible*

"There is nothing better than coorie-ing down to a good book, cosy in cashmere with a stiff, salty gin in hand (Harris, of course!). Gabriella Bennett plugs you straight into the most stylish of Scottish lifestyle trends. Everyone in Alba knows how to do a cracking coorie, and for the rest of the world this guide will have you native in no time."
Lynne Coleman, author of *The Fashion Annual*

"*The Art of Coorie* shows it is possible to be sumptuous and simple at the same time. A gem of a book that offers a new perspective on Scotland."
Louise Welsh, author of *The Cutting Room*

"Find herein Gabriella catapulting coorie aw over Scotland's cultural cosmos and realms beyond. Out of a seedling of Scots sprouts fun, factual and gallus text that's the right measures of many 'hings: historical enough, sartorial enough, culinary enough, landscape and natural enough, objects enough, festive enough, boozy enough, lush enough fur sure. With stunning imagery, a cap doffed to literary leaders and paragoning songsmiths, plus a playlist to boot, it's an enchanting and interactive read."
Michael Pedersen, poet and curator of *Neu! Reekie!*

"Gabriella Bennett's book on the cult of 'coorie' – a hug of a word – is a celebration of all that's best and beautiful about Scotland, from food to textiles, pubs to gardens. It made this Scottish émigré miss my homeland, its wildness and drama and warmth, with a physical pang. But I will never embrace the midge."
Marina O'Loughlin, journalist, author and restaurant critic

The Art of Coorie

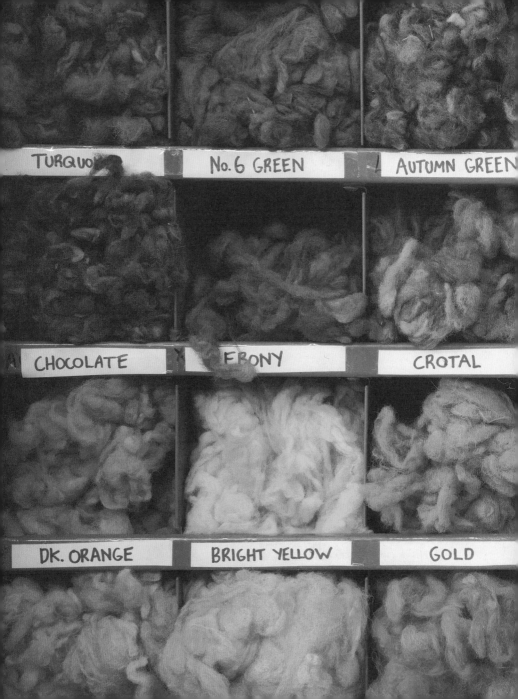

KHAKI JUB. BROWN MAPLE

COUNTRY CROTAL LT. TAN LT. ORANGE

RYE STRAW LT. MAPLE

The Art of Coorie

How to Live Happy the Scottish Way

GABRIELLA BENNETT

BLACK & WHITE PUBLISHING

First published 2018
by Black & White Publishing Ltd
Nautical House, 104 Commercial Street,
Edinburgh, EH6 6NF

1 3 5 7 9 10 8 6 5 4 2   18 19 20 21

ISBN: 978 1 78530 181 0

A CIP catalogue record is available from the British Library.

Cover photography © Anna Lamotte at Guardswell Farm
Endpaper photography © Mairi Helena Fabrics & Wallpapers

Design by Craig Gallacher
Printed and bound in Turkey by Imago

COORIE / kuːri / >
noun [mass noun]

1   The Scottish art of deriving comfort,
    wellbeing and energy from wild landscapes
    and convivial interiors.
2   "A hug of a word."

INFORMAL an affectionate nestle into a loved one
SEE ALSO the old Gaelic *còsagach* "snug or cosy"

Contents

1. COORIE BEGINS 1

2. CHALLENGES TO COORIE 21

3. COORIE COMMANDMENTS 35

4. COORIE WORDS 45

5. COORIE TRADITIONS 53

6. WILD COORIE 65

7. COORIE IN THE CITY 85

8. COORIE CAMPING 105

9. THE COORIE PUB 121

10. COORIE GARDENS 131

11. COORIE FOOD AND DRINK 149

12. COORIE TEXTILES 163

13. COORIE STYLE 177

14. THE MAKERS OF COORIE 191

15. COORIE HIDEOUTS 205

16. THRIFTY COORIE 229

17. FESTIVE COORIE 249

18. COORIE CONTINUES 261

Coorie Begins 1

It wasn't so long ago the word "coorie" meant something else. In Scotland, you know you're in good company when a friend or family member pats a small space on their couch and invites you to "coorie in". Squashed in next to them, you might not have an awful lot of room but at least you're snug.

Coorie has long been synonymous with nestling affectionately into a loved one, but only recently has it entered everyday parlance as a way to describe a scene. One equally warm and comforting, where a cosy room lit by a flickering fire provides refuge from the banshee wind and horizontal rain outside.

The art of coorie has been around for hundreds of years, yet summing up the essence of Scottishness in a single term has always proved elusive. Now we can put both word and concept together to give us a comfortable manifesto for living.

Coorie is a word I've come to associate with the warmth and geniality of Glaswegians. I was born on England's south coast and, although I grew up in Fife, it was in Glasgow where I first heard the word coorie used, first by my friends and then, later, in its new incarnation, through my work as a lifestyle journalist.

When talking with interior designers I began to hear coorie as a word used to describe Scottish homes with sheepskin-covered sofas and log-burning stoves where people wanted to spend time with each other. When I put this new usage to Scots textile artists and makers, they seemed excited. They spoke passionately about how they had long searched for a word that described their work; one that referenced their Scottish heritage yet implied a contemporary spin. Maybe, they told me, they could borrow the word coorie to illustrate their creativity.

It soon became clear that coorie reflected a wider lifestyle. The idea can be applied to almost every aspect of life: from buying clothes that reinvent traditional Scottish materials, to eating food grown in Lairg or the Borders, to exploring the country's hidden nooks and enjoying outdoor adventures.

These objects and experiences can be obviously Scottish or more covertly so. Building them into our lives gives us an understanding of where we come from and where we're going. Coorie also allows us to surround ourselves with lovely things – DIY projects, treasures from nature or items created by the ever-growing collective of Scottish makers.

THE COORIE IDEAL

The ideal coorie scene should reflect a balance of the outside and in. Bring to mind a day spent Munro-bagging or loch swimming, bookended by a bowl of something hot and nourishing as you dry off next to a heat source with a contented dog at your side. Don't forget smell: faint lanolin clinging to woollen blankets, cinnamon dissolving into porridge cooking slowly on the hob, the frosty pinch of winter air when you step into a Trossachs morning. If a King Creosote album is playing as you road trip across the humpbacked north-west Highlands then all the better. The more homegrown ingredients are added to the mix, the coorier life will be.

Coorie's newfound role has been helped along by the fact it is a beautiful word. Derived from Old Scots, there is something soothing about the look, sound and shape of coorie: soft in the mouth and easy for both natives and non-natives to pronounce. A kind of dove's trill for the human tongue.

Experts agree. James Robertson, the Scots language author, says that coorie has the same origins as the word "cower", and its etymology can be traced back via the Old Norse word "kura".

"It has a variety of meanings," Robertson

says. "In Robert Burns' poem 'Tam o' Shanter', when the poet admits that words fail him in describing the dancing of Nannie the witch, he writes:

> But here my Muse her wing maun cour,
> Sic flights are far beyond her power."

Here, "cour" means to bend or fold. But in 'The Twa Doos', a song by the eighteenth-century Scottish baroness Lady Nairne, it means "cover":

> The snaw will come an' cour the grund,
> Nae grains o' wheat will then be fund.

In its longer form, however, coorie or "courie" traditionally implied activity.

Robertson says, "A tall person might coorie doon in order to go through a low doorway, or a village might coorie in the shelter of a hill. It's in this sense, cuddling or nestling in to something or someone, that 'coorie' – usually followed by *in* or *doon* – is most widely used today."

Robertson also believes coorie is especially relevant in the winter when it suggests shelter. "When it's cold, wet and windy outside, and night has fallen, there's nothing better than to be cooried in by the fireside," he adds.

ATTENTION TURNS NORTH

Others soon picked up on coorie's new definition. At the end of 2017, in the months preceding coorie breaking through into the mainstream, VisitScotland announced its travel predictions for the following year.

It tipped "còsagach", similar to coorie, as a trend. The Gaelic word loosely translates to mean cosy; the tourist board encourages visitors staying in Highland log cabins to get comfy beside a roaring fire with a book, a hot toddy and good friends.

For some, this idea was a shade too close to the lifestyles our Nordic cousins have been exporting in recent years. Hygge and lagom, the Danish and Swedish movements of living well, have proved some of Northern Europe's most marketable concepts, even if we're not entirely sure how to pronounce them.

But while these movements laid the groundwork for a similar trend to emerge in Scotland, coorie has some obvious differences.

Where hygge is concerned with the pursuit of happiness through candles, coffee and togetherness, coorie seeks to make the most of what comes from Scotland to feel satisfied.

Lagom is the art of balancing frugality and fairness to create a balanced existence. Coorie takes into account being kind to the earth and our wallets, but can also extend to premium experiences once in a while.

Crucially, neither of these Scandinavian lifestyle approaches took their starting point from what is dug out of the earth. Coorie is more than simply being cosy. Sure, it is linked, but more importantly it focuses on working out how to be in tune with our surroundings to evoke that feeling.

The new coorie represents a way of life where peacefulness comes from engaging with our heritage, be it in tiny ways or on a grander scale. Life can be harsh in a country's most isolated locations, but *The Art of Coorie* explores how ingenuity has been born from extreme conditions.

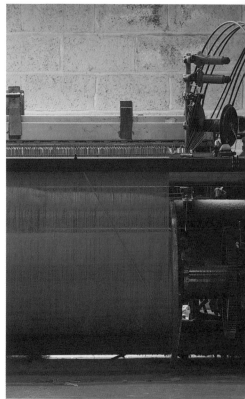

WE ARE WHAT WE BUY

Research took me to Scotland's furthest outposts and back into the heartlands to find the people who live and breathe coorie. Textile designers updating clan tweeds for historic country estates told me about their business vision – one that features global reference points but always stays true to an inherently Scottish ethos. Young chefs who swapped careers in Denmark to start a pioneering food studio in Edinburgh showed me how the dishes they serve came from the land around them. They illustrate coorie credentials writ large.

It's apparent that consumers in pursuit of a more mindful life are looking within Scotland to find a new way forward, partly because of the appealing backstory attached to products, but also thanks to the quality of what they are buying. The demand for commission-led pieces that take time and skill to create hasn't been stronger since the days of making all garments and furniture by hand. These days, Scotland's zeitgeist calls for a return to "slow goods", replacing the fast consumerism of the nineties and noughties.

Even so, the coorie lifestyle is nothing new.

Scots have cultivated a reputation for resourcefulness over hundreds of years. Before he invented the telephone, Alexander Graham Bell created a device for his family's farm that dehusked wheat with a set of nail brushes. While Bell didn't contend with the logistics of running a small business from a remote Scottish island, he did know how to think laterally. The result was a solution that afforded a simpler and more fulfilling life – exactly what coorie embodies.

Coorie also takes into account the unique trials of living in Scotland. Instead of allowing the weather or the geography to shape our lives in negative ways, coorie harnesses these challenges.

THE THREE CHIMNEYS OF SKYE

Thirty years ago, when Shirley Spear and her husband, Eddie, opened a restaurant on the Isle of Skye, there was little choice but to use what was around them. At that time there was no bridge to connect the island with mainland Scotland and it was tricky to access the resources needed to overhaul a modest cottage into a fine dining establishment.

Thanks to a little imagination and a great deal of enterprising spirit, the Three Chimneys is now considered one of Scotland's best restaurants with rooms. Its success lies in two key ideas – locality and simplicity.

It just so happens that coorie is one of Shirley's favourite words.

"The word coorie, or coorie doon, means a great deal more to me as a Scot than *còsagach*," she says. "It is one I relate to cuddling or snuggling up, and it also means to squat down or bend low, in relation to getting down on your haunches to a low place – something I struggle with more and more these days! There is a lovely old song – a lullaby about 'coorie doon my deeri'. And I still haven't managed to work out how to pronounce *còsagach*."

WHAT'S IN A NUMBER?

It doesn't cost a lot of money to be coorie. In fact, much of the time the opposite is true. High society pursuits often don't fit with the concept – it's hard to work out how to shoehorn coorie into a trip to the opera, save for bringing a spoon whittled from Scots pine to stir your Martini during the interval.

That said, a raft of high-end places show how to do coorie beautifully. They have reflected their Scottish environment through their offerings and tempt travellers from around the globe. There is no shame in balancing this with the thrifty side of coorie.

PEAK COSY?

Of course, it can be tricky to convince everyone to get on board with the trend. Complaints about coorie centre on arguments that encouraging superfluous spending is irresponsible, and that the world has already achieved "peak cosy".

Here's how I see it. Nearly all of us have a chunk of disposable income to spend every year. Highlighting ways to live better won't solve climate change or reverse governmental cuts, but they can amp up our – and others' – quality of life.

As for scorn poured on the cosy brigade, show me a man wearing a Fair Isle jumper who isn't happy with life and I'll show you an extremely warm liar. As long as people endure long winters they'll search for a way to withstand inclement weather, especially if this can be done through a creative hobby such as knitting.

Coorie isn't concerned with spending cash needlessly. It doesn't want you to empty your purse and wait until the next trend comes around then entice you to do it all over again. Coorie is about making the best of the time and money you have with innovative ideas. If Scotland has been best known for whisky, tartan and shortbread until now, it's time to lift the lid on new talent and add ceramics, sneakers and sourdough to that list.

With a bit of luck, you'll find ideas on these pages for kit you'd already planned to buy. Recipes that revive familiar ingredients, recommendations for eating out at places that might not have been on your radar, and holidays on home soil are all covered. Coorie doesn't want you to forget about travelling abroad. I'll take you along to the best locations in Scotland and let you make up your own mind about where you want to go next.

Show me a man wearing a Fair Isle jumper who isn't happy with life and I'll show you an extremely warm liar.

COORIE FOR ALL

Scots are an inquisitive bunch. They ask questions, pick over the finer details and want counter-arguments backed up. Sometimes there can be wariness of the unknown. Coorie offers a familiar newness, a fresh take on an old word extolling the virtues of things we have always known. This time, instead of endlessly trawling the internet bookmarking makers, ingredients and trips, *The Art of Coorie* has neatly rounded up everything you might need in eighteen chapters.

Coorie may have started life in Scotland but it's a philosophy that can be adapted to any country and employed by any nationality. You don't have to be a mountaineering expert or a budding interior designer to get on board with the idea. Who cares that your wardrobe is a mess, or your home doesn't look like glossy decor magazines? Don't tell anyone, but neither does mine.

WHERE NEXT?

On these pages are ruminations on identity past and present. There are tips for every budget and level of interest. The key to a coorie life is right in front of us – all that's needed is the desire to build on an awareness of Scotland. So, get ready to jump in. **c**

Challenges to Coorie   2

It's easy to identify tourists on Edinburgh's Royal Mile. They're the ones bound in knitted scarves, wearing puffa jackets and woolly hats no matter the time of year. When the wind whistles around the New Town's handsome Georgian streets, their stoic faces show the effort of turning away from its bite.

But is Scotland's climate really so inhospitable? Glasgow can be uncommonly dreich, smirr blurring the architectural mishmash of the city's skyline. The east coast plays host to some truly cruel gales, eroding the sharp edges off fishermen's cottages in Fife and Angus.

In the winter months it can feel like the country takes any opportunity to grind to a halt. The faintest threat of snow causes chaos across road, rail and air. Transport Scotland's army of gritting lorries can be tracked via an app; each has its own identity. If you live in Ayrshire you may see Luke Snowwalker at the end of your street. Sirs Salter Scott and Andy Flurry are the doyens of the crew.

HOME TRUTHS

Perhaps we live in a wilder place than we give ourselves credit for. Scots tend to be hardy perennials. It's as if we've evolved to withstand the challenging nature of our own country. And, what's more, we've worked out how to shape it into a force for good. Out of necessity our homes feature clever ways to keep the outside out and the inside warm. Scotland's oldest towerhouses were built with slits for windows not just as a defensive measure, but to protect residents from the elements. Out of problems came solutions, even beauty. Our foreparents thought to install open fires to heat their homes then toiled to make them easy on the eye. Intricately carved wooden fireplaces and elaborate stone hearths that referenced Scottish folklore followed.

There is scant evidence to back up the idea that Scots spend more time inside than inhabitants of other countries, but the theory makes sense. We spend prolonged periods in pubs and restaurants after all, whiling away the hours with friends, waiting in vain for the weather to ease. Our homes become a natural extension of these convivial spaces: warm and open to guests. Spending so much time indoors with other people, perhaps over an alcoholic drink, encourages conversation, arguments and resolutions. It fills us up with more knowledge – or at least allows us to realise there are other opinions aside from our own.

TRANSFORMING HOMES

Studies suggest that Scots spend less on home decor than anywhere else in the UK, but what we do spend big on is renovating and converting our properties instead of moving house. Property experts have attributed this recent phenomenon to the knock-on effect of the Scottish government raising the rate of land and buildings transaction tax, a tiered levy applied to homes that cost more than £145,000. Planning bodies in Edinburgh and Glasgow have seen the number of change-of-use applications soar in recent times, in particular for the transformation of commercial property into private residences, and the extension of existing homes.

Instead of moving home and incurring extra tax, it appears homeowners prefer to line the pockets of Scotland's architects. This suggests that instead of seeing the politics of home ownership and house building as a problem, we are choosing to turn it into an

opportunity. This shift in thinking can help us live more comfortably, be more in touch with our individual needs, and in turn support Scottish practitioners.

It also negates the cliché of Scots as stingy: the last to get a round in at the bar, the first to pull out a calculator and divvy up a bill instead of footing it ourselves. Earnings have failed to rise in line with inflation for the vast majority of the UK's residents. This we know. The reality is that we are worse off financially than we have ever been. Yet our incomes are still being spent. Just on different aspects of our lives.

A REBIRTH IN PROVENANCE

Research compiled by Travelodge showed that trips abroad fell by 18 per cent in the years that followed the 2008 recession. The data also revealed that the number of Brits choosing to holiday at home rose by almost 6 per cent in the same period, suggesting that during times of economic uncertainty people look to comforting, familiar treats. Meanwhile, the must-haves we're encouraged to lust over bombard us from every direction. Jewellery. Clothes. Technology. Cars. In pursuit of them, the reasons for which we are enticed to buy slip from view. To make life happier, to have more downtime and fewer complications.

These notions underpin the coorie movement. Folk practising the coorie commandments are working to cast aside fast consumerism and usher in meaningful products. One school of thought argues that handing a population the information they need to make decisions on

how to live a more mindful existence is half the battle. In this instance, it's hard to deny the influence of political shift. It's clear to see that the independence referendum re-energised Scotland and forced us to equip ourselves with facts and well-informed opinions like never before. Knowledge became the must-have accessory of 2014. Some claim the referendum divided the country, but there are signs it sparked a collective sense of consciousness too.

Scots have woken up to what goes into their minds, their food and their homes. They want better. Some say Scottish identity has always been governed by the same factors: as a nation we have long faced turmoil and played the underdog more times than we care to remember. But we have also repeatedly overcome. And thrived.

SCOTLAND AND THE ARTS

It is no coincidence that some of the world's most outstanding creative talent was born in Scotland. Glasgow is home to more Turner Prize nominees and winners than any other UK location. A stream of poets flows out of every village and city. Our video game designers have exported their ideas to distant shores.

Dundee – once considered the small, shabby sister to Glasgow and Edinburgh – is now home to the only V&A museum outside of London. Its geometric form appears washed up from the River Tay like mirrored jetsam, but Philip Long, the museum's director, believes its stake in the story of Dundee runs deeper than simple aesthetics.

Belle and Sebastian – 'Electronic Renaissance'

"After decades of difficult years and uncertain times, Dundee is now a city that really is transforming," Long told the *Architects' Journal*. "Scotland has an extraordinarily rich design heritage and continues to lead the way with creative and inspiring innovations. There are many, many designers and manufacturers creating impeccably crafted new products, services and life-changing innovations."

Joanna Norman, director of the V&A research institute, agrees. "The influence of Scottish design is not limited to one country, it has been felt around the world," she adds. "I think those who visit will be surprised and intrigued to learn about the impact this relatively small country has, and continues to have, on the world of design."

THE SHIFTING OF SHAPES

It seems the world is beginning to take notice of Scotland's more recent achievements. Yet this progression raises another question. What drives people living in a small country amid austere times to produce such incredible work? Perhaps the answer lies in considering what surrounds the places where this work is made.

When we listen to music we don't just hear the noises a performer wants us to. What we really hear is how the sound lives temporarily in the space we are in and where it was captured. Some of the first guests at Scotland's only Airbnb bookshop were members of The Bookshop Band. The act's members, who write songs inspired by books, recorded an EP during their stay at the £36-a-night Open Book in Wigtown, Dumfries and Galloway, vying for space with titles on wild birds and archaeology. Listeners are hearing the shape of the shop as well as the instruments and vocals.

The same idea applies to art. A portrait can change its character depending on where it is placed and what light it receives. In his early career the artist John Lowrie Morrison – known as Jolomo – smoked cigars in a bid to ward off midges when painting landscapes outside in Argyll. Eventually defeated by their bites, he was forced to move to an indoor studio – something he now credits with making his work more accomplished. The spaces around us define so much more of our lives than we might at first think.

And so the Scottish nature unfurls. Edwin Morgan, the Glasgow-born poet, imposed harsh structure on much of his work. In his book of poetry, *Glasgow Sonnets*, he revised the age-old poetic constraint and added a sharp local twist. Apply restrictions on people with vision and their desire to make doesn't just endure. It flourishes.

OVERCOMING ADVERSITY, THE COORIE WAY

Even accessing the materials makers need to hone their craft can be difficult. Scottish urbanites are better connected than ever before, but great swathes of the country still receive a raw deal from supermarkets, retailers and suppliers who impose punitive surcharges to deliver goods and roll out services simply because they live in outlying areas.

These people didn't get mad – they got even. In fact, they got better than even.

On a collection of over one hundred islands flung far out between the Atlantic Ocean and the North Sea, Shetlanders have worked out how to make what they need by using what is locally available. In bygone years islanders wove taatits – sturdy rugs that doubled as bedcovers – and Fair Isle jumpers with wool from island sheep. Their legend has inspired foreign weavers to up sticks and continue the tradition on Shetland soil. Inspired, haute couture fashion houses from around the world have since turned their attention to Scotland's most northern archipelago.

Gourmands from all over the globe are checking out Scotland for ingredients that once filled the dinner bowls of serfs. They dine on dishes using seaweed, pine needles and peasemeal in ways that turn the perception of Scotland as a nation of deep-fried Mars bar lovers on its head.

Coorie isn't just a decorative extra. Amid trying circumstances, Scots and honorary Scots have dug deep and fought through. They have also asked people close by for help. The result of these collaborations is a country greater than the sum of its parts, a bothy in the storm offering shelter through shared ideas and homage paid to the past. You only need to knock on the door. c

Coorie is a way of being that
takes in what's around us.

Coorie Commandments 3

1. THOU SHALT RESPECT SCOTLAND'S HISTORY ... BUT NOT BECOME A PASTICHE

Tartan? Sure. Tin of shortbread? Absolutely. But not always in the ways the world expects. Tradition is a dish best served fresh, so instead of perpetuating tired stereotypes of Scotland, the coorie movement moves forward our oldest rituals.

The cooriest among us are giving notions from the past a reboot and we can follow their lead across art, craft, food and home. They know it isn't about being Scottish before all else. Many choose to identify as a Scot second and a creative person first, because nationality is only a single thread woven into their story.

For example, designers are continuing tweed and tartan production but in bold new directions. These fabrics were originally used to create clothing that provided an income for remote communities. Now they are being rejuvenated in ways that root Scotland in the context of global fashion.

2. THOU SHALL NOT FEAR THE COLD

It is a little known fact that all Scots are born with a built-in radiator to get them through winter. It's called a hipflask, and we aren't afraid to fill it. In lieu of this, the key is layers. So many coorie activities involve being outdoors: hiking demands a steely core and constitution, exploring the woods for crafty finds requires sturdy footwear – even skiing in the Cairngorms requires patience. All these pursuits offer the chance to clear the mind and get to know the country from within.

Wild swimming in Scottish lochs is having a moment. A recent surge in popularity at events

such as the Great Scottish Swim has seen record numbers and increased membership at open water swimming clubs. Its beauty, swimmers claim, lies in the restorative nature of an ice-cold dip set against a backdrop of Scotland's most idyllic scenery. Nobody promised Barbadian temperatures, or clear blue seas, but for enthusiasts the appeal lies in testing yourself to your furthest limits. Wild swimming with other like-minded souls not only ensures your safety in remote locations, but also gives you a buddy to motivate you through the initial bone-chilling shock of the water.

3. THOU SHALL KEEP IT SCOTTISH (WHERE POSSIBLE)

Running a small business is now more difficult than ever. The convenience of online shopping, coupled with the "death of the high street" (has there ever been a more overused headline?), has turned people away from seeking out independent stores from which to buy gifts and groceries.

But we know that the ripple effect of local business people doing well spreads throughout the whole community. A prosperous town centre filled with independent shops has been found to significantly increase house prices. The social function plays a vital role, too: bookshops, cafés and restaurants that host a diverse range of events provide a much-needed space valuable to different demographics.

Local councils have a long way to go to make our high streets a financially viable place to set up shop, but subsidised stall fees at planned events are a good start.

It's not even as lofty as buying from farmers' markets or eating organic. The food writer Ruby Tandoh explores the joys of the local corner shop, describing them as "technicolour temples" with their rows of tinned goodies, jars of old-fashioned sweets and garish packaging.

One of my favourite local corner shops, found during years of renting flats in Glasgow, is a

> "To me it means to snuggle in or huddle in. Coorie in if the kids are going to bed, and coorie doon if it's cold."

bright yellow convenience store in St George's Cross where the cheery shopkeeper finds a way to segue a terrible joke into all transactions. Standing in the phosphorescent glow of his backlit fridges while choosing a tin of fizzy juice, I always knew my hangover was on its way out.

Money in the pocket of small businesses is cash that helps local people and their families. The idea isn't to phase out the big retailers altogether. Anyone who promotes that isn't really in tune with the workings of everyday life. Instead, it's about making tiny improvements where we can, in the hope that they add up to a significant difference.

4. THOU SHALL ATTEMPT A STAYCATION, EVEN IF THOU DETESTS THE WORD STAYCATION

There are two types of people in the world. Those who will camp, and those who won't. Those who fall into the former category need

little encouragement to pack up their sleeping bag and a Kelly Kettle and head out into the countryside. Those in the latter camp, myself included, might benefit from the incentive of some coorie camping ideas (see chapter 8).

Scotland's Land Reform Act 2003 comes down firmly on the side of responsible campers. The ones who wander freely clearing up after themselves can set up a tent anywhere they fancy, as long as they show respect. This freedom to roam also lends itself well to the coorie movement. Braving the night-time chill around a fire with a furry friend at your feet and a hot chocolate in your hands after a day of toiling to create a coorie campsite is pretty special.

Research proves that we like to holiday in Scotland, but it is important to note too the wider economic influences at play.

Scotland's financial trade body noted a marked decrease in Brits' overseas spending in 2017. The weak pound, inflation and uncertainty over Brexit were cited as reasons, but it feels short-sighted to say that the taste for global

> "Coorie is to feel included, warm and cosy. For reading a book together or telling stories. Fire on, as well."

travel has dissipated altogether. Instead, it feels like an opportunity for sniffing out beautiful places at home has arisen, one that combines short-stay trips with longer-haul plans abroad. A caravan stay in Aberfeldy is a more realistic option for the extended family than schlepping abroad en masse. Bonding time between grandparents and wee ones also gives mums and dads the chance for a gin on the banks of the River Tay before sundown.

5. THOU MUST SET THE SCENE WITH TUNES

Ever started a long car journey and realised you forgot to make a playlist? Me too. I'm not maligning Simple minds, but there are only so many times their greatest hits can be played in a confined space without civil unrest breaking out.

Road trips aren't the only time a decent playlist is required. How we consume music has changed radically over the years. Dinner at my grandparents' house was set to silence, at my parents' the radio, and at my friends' something much more personal: a playlist put together for the occasion with songs that are meaningful to us.

Supper is on hold until the right music starts to play, even if it means holding a knife and fork and slavering over the smell of dinner until the person in charge of the tunes has done their job.

6. EMBRACE THE MIDGE

Everyone has a theory on what attracts the Highland midge to certain people. What can be agreed upon is that these minuscule biting insects are the greatest hindrance to enjoying life outdoors in Scotland.

Not to be confused with mosquitoes, the midge is most common in the western Highlands, Islands, and Argyll – in fact, any location where water meets land. They prefer acidic soils, peaty and rich in nutrients, and dance over rushes and reeds in a fast-paced mating ritual.

God help anyone who walks through a cloud of midges. Bites are more often than not painless – it is only days later when the skin rises in angry red bumps that the midge's poison takes its itchy hold. Worse still, the midge seems to be immune to extreme weather. Like some kind of dystopian sci-fi movie, Scotland's "big freeze" winter of 2010 did not so much decrease the midge population as increase it, since animals such as bats were killed and the midge found itself predator-free.

Science suggests some people are more attractive to the midge because of the taste of their blood. When the London School of Hygiene and Tropical Medicine completed trials on participants living in the Scottish Highlands, researchers deduced that the blood of subjects with the fewest numbers of bites contained high

levels of ketone, a chemical produced when the body burns fat. The data will help to develop a drug to repel the midge and the disease-harbouring mosquito altogether.

In the meantime, solutions are limited. People swear by a range of options, from eating Marmite sandwiches to Avon's Skin So Soft, a citronella body spray. A hat with a net to cover the face is the best way to block the midge from skin access altogether, but you're at serious risk of a Hannibal Lector aesthetic. Personally, I think it's worth running the gamut of midges to sip at least one hot drink on the patio.

7. THOU MUST SHARE IDEAS – AND SPREAD THE WORD

The bookshop that offers a box at the till with a sign saying "Free books! Help yourself" will always win favour over its competitors. In my research for The Art of Coorie it became clear that the giving and swapping of goods and labour in creative industries functions as a crucial currency.

It's a message that forms the bedrock of coorie. Bakery47, the now defunct but hugely popular café in Glasgow's Southside, offered a weekly "bread barter" where customers could take away a loaf of sourdough in exchange for an hour of their time or the offer to repair a broken object on the premises.

One of the best parts of meeting makers through my job is finding that they were only too keen to tell me about other people whose work they rated. Far from seeing them as competition, their excitement grew when they talked about a new collaborative project or meeting, a kind of Venn diagram where the overlapping of two disciplines created something fresh and precious.

There is an understandable desire to want to keep nice things to ourselves. But isn't there also a responsibility to share what we find? Social media fosters a need to tell the world what we are doing at all times, especially if it supports the notion that what we are doing is exciting. But what's on our screens also lets us find out about new restaurants, shops and artists, especially when we live hundreds of miles away. Twitter and Instagram are opening up Scotland to the rest of the world. The internet as a force for good – it really is possible. c

Coorie Words 4

The closest book most journalists have to a bible is their publication's style guide. Looking back over previous editions allows us to track the "ebb and flow of a living language", according to *The Times*. In my eyes, new additions to a style guide or dictionary highlight the impact of shifts in culture better than almost anything else.

One of my friends has synaesthesia, a condition where one sense automatically triggers another; in her case it means she sees words as colours. I find this endlessly fascinating, and to a lesser degree I think this switch from one sense to a second happens to us all when describing the country around us. Say the word "whisky" and you immediately call to mind bulbous copper pot stills glinting in the belly of Ardbeg distillery on Islay. Or at least I do.

In order to get a true sense of Scotland you first have to learn the vernacular. Words with roots in Lallans and Doric, the dialects of the lowlands and north east, sing with history. Words are readily borrowed and redistributed between the country's three languages, Gaelic, Scots and English.

Lots of Scots (and non-Scots) tell me coorie ranks highly in their list of favourite words. There are many more that paint a picture of Scotland at its cooriest. Here are a few of the best.

"Your daddy coories doon, my darling,

Doon in a three foot seam,

So you can coorie doon my darling,

Coorie doon and dream."

The Miner's Lullaby, traditional song

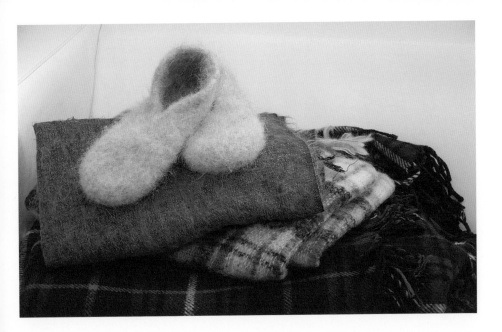

BAFFIES

Noun

Slippers.

"I've got my baffies on and I've stuck a log on the fire – we're in for a cosy night."

BAM

Noun

Someone displaying stupidity.

"You've put your stovies in the oven but not turned the heat on, ya bam!"

BLETHER

Verb

To engage in a long chat or gossip.

"We sat in the sun on our lunch break and started to blether."

BRAW

Adjective

Pleasing to the eye or person.

"You're looking braw in that scarf, hen."

CLAP

Verb

The act of petting or stroking an animal.

"Hi pal, can I clap your dug?"

CLOSE

Noun

The communal stairwell in tenement flats or other shared residential buildings.

"Did you see the plants number four put out in the close? Makes it look braw."

DREICH

Adjective

Wet, soggy weather conditions with grey skies and cold temperatures.

"It's dreich in Invergarry today, better bring your waterproofs for the walk to school."

DROOKET

Adjective

Soaking wet from the rain.

"I'm so drooket even my pants are wet."

GALLUS

Adjective

Bold, adventurous. Also used to describe a pristine setting or person.

"Let's keep the garden looking gallus."
"That was gallus of Mairi to tackle Ben Nevis after necking a Harris gin and tonic."

GUTTIES

Noun

Plimsoll-type shoes.

"I went in the river with my gutties on cos I was feart of the rocks."

HOUSECOAT / GOONY

Noun

Dressing gown.

"Maw, my housecoat's gone walkabout!"

JUICE

Noun

Any beverage aside from H_2O, hot drinks or alcohol.

"I opened a tin of juice to cool down after my hike but I've spilled it everywhere."

MESSAGES

Noun

Groceries or general shopping.

"I'm needing to head into town to pick up some messages for the kids' tea."

MOORIE-CAVIE

Noun; Shetland

A blizzard of fine, powdery snow.

"It's blawin' a moorie-cavie oot der."

PEELY WALLY

Adjective

Extremely pale.

"Should have seen the nick of Finlay after a night out in Glasgow. He was peely wally and needing a tin of juice."

PIECE

Noun

Sandwich.

"Away and make your wee brother a piece and jam for his lunch."

QUINE

Noun; Doric

Girl or young woman.

> "The quine at the bus stop told me the 37 was on its way – I'll be home for my tea soon."

RIDDY / BEAMER

Noun

A face red with embarrassment.

> "Colin couldn't get the campfire started last night. Should have seen his beamer."

SHOOGLE

Verb

To shake or rattle something back and forth.

> "If your key's stuck in the lock, give it a wee shoogle to get it free."

SWALLY

Noun

A small sip.

> "Give us a swally of your whisky, pal."

YALDI

Noun

A triumphant exclamation.

> "I took my boots off without undoing the laces. Yaldi!" **c**

Coorie Traditions 5

Scots love a get-together, so it's no surprise that our traditions call for high levels of debauchery. But they are also a time to remember our ancestors and make new memories with loved ones. These are some of our most enduring customs.

UP HELLY AA

What is coorier than celebrating life with a huge bonfire in the coldest month of the year? For those who look forward to Up Helly Aa, the annual paean to Shetland's Viking connections, not much.

On the last Tuesday of January, the townsfolk of Lerwick, Shetland's capital, take twenty-four hours out of their calendar to drink, sing, and be merry in the name of their ancestors. In this sub-arctic archipelago, where the land's latitude is aligned with southern Greenland, nothing can stop their fun. Since the 1880s, when the festival began, only a few events have stopped Up Helly Aa from running. None were weather-related.

The festival's chief, known as the Guizer Jarl, braves all conditions to delight thousands of visitors with his outfit, a carefully kept secret until the day of the festival. Come night, a flaming line of guizers snakes its way through the town, culminating in its arrival at a huge Viking ship, the product of four months' work. The ship is then set alight to the rhythmic beat of drums.

In some ways, Shetlanders' traditions have become fossilised because of this annual dedication. In others, Up Helly Aa shows how the islands are adapting to Scotland's shifting nature. More recently there has been debate about why women cannot be part of the procession in Lerwick, where the conversation about gender remains a sensitive subject. Guizers have always been men, but there are calls to haul this particular aspect of the historic tradition into the twenty-first century.

HOGMANAY

Scotland has a long love affair with parties. Hogmanay, our souped-up version of New Year, began as a marking of the winter solstice, when people would show their gratitude for the end of the long, dark nights on the year's shortest day.

In many parts of Scotland, Hogmanay is a bigger deal than Christmas. Having served as an alternative for so many centuries when yuletide was banned under Protestant rule, Hogmanay parties are louder and more richly ingrained in the cultural landscape than those of our English neighbours.

The week bookended by Christmas and Hogmanay has become a calendric no man's land, where eating, drinking and socialising form a calorie-laden holy trinity. Snacks are the saviour and no one knows quite what day it is. Instead it is easier to ping from each of the important dates: the last day of work, Christmas Eve, New Year's Day, and then back into the office, growing heavier and more fatigued at each step, but filled up with family time and friendship.

The etymology of Hogmanay is more difficult to discern. One theory is that the word entered Middle Scots, the language spoken by Lowlanders between 1450 and 1700, because of the French. Taken from the northern French dialectal word *hoguinané*, which in turn was influenced by the sixteenth-century Middle French word *aguillanneuf*, the day is thought to reference a gift that is given, often to children, at new year.

Dr Donna Heddle, the director of the Institute for Northern Studies at the University of the Highlands and Islands, says that Hogmanay first entered the vocabulary following the return of Mary Queen of Scots to her homeland in 1561.

"The name could also come from the Anglo-Saxon *haleg monath* meaning holy month," Dr Heddle says. "But the most likely source seems to be French. In Normandy presents given at Hogmanay were *hoguignetes*."

Come Hogmanay, a few superstitions are supposed to be upheld. Immediately after the stroke of midnight, also known as the bells, a rousing version of *Auld Lang Syne* should be sung, even if not everyone knows the words.

A recent study revealed that only 3 per cent of the British population can recite a word-perfect rendition of the Robert Burns classic, rising to 7 per cent of Scots. Only half of the population know it was written by Scotland's national bard. Tragically, or brilliantly, depending on where you stand on 1990s superstars, 3 per cent think the song was written by Mariah Carey.

After the song, a glass of something should be poured while partygoers circulate and distribute a hug, kiss and best wishes to all guests for the year ahead.

FIRST-FOOTING

First-footing is a second post-bells tradition. The story goes that the first guest over a house's threshold should be a tall, dark man holding a symbolic object: a coin, a lump of coal, shortbread, black bun (a type of dense, sweet cake), or a bottle of whisky. All represent prosperity for the coming months. The patron's colouring is believed to be another throwback to Viking times. If a blonde, bearded stranger arrived at your door without warning, the underlying message would be one of alarm rather than goodwill.

Scotland is the only country within the UK to
bestow upon its citizens a national holiday on both
the first and second of January. It takes a while to
recover from that glass of something.

THE LOONY DOOK

In reality, the majority of Scots don't always observe festive customs nowadays. But one tradition that many still enjoy is the loony dook. On New Year's Day, bold souls head down to water – most famously the Firth of Forth, off South Queensferry – to swim in freezing temperatures and raise money for charity. More than a thousand swimmers, known as loonies, take their dook, or dip, clad in fancy dress. The loony dook tradition is only about thirty years old, but has emerged as one of the most attention-grabbing customs of the festive period. Scottish newspapers are sure to feature images of the year's dook on the front page of their editions for January the second, especially if bathers are dressed outlandishly.

A PORTION OF STEAK PIE

Steak pie on New Year's night is another staple. This stodgy meal soaks up any remnants of alcohol in the system and also acts as a quick and easy dinner, especially if the pie is pre-bought – and you've been working up an appetite with your loony dook earlier in the day. Historically, family heads often had to work on the first of January, so a steak pie bought from the butcher was considered a good way to offer a filling meal that took little time to prepare. Settling down with a portion of steak pie and a mountain of clap shot (potato and turnip mash) in front of the TV is coorie bliss on the first day of the New Year.

BURNS NIGHT

If steak pie acts as the culinary talisman of Hogmanay, haggis represents a similar idea for Burns Night. The annual celebration of Scotland's most famous poet brings with it a raft of tropes fixated on eating but also on ways to encourage healthy discourse.

Exactly a month after Christmas Day, a supper is held to commemorate Burns' contribution to the literary landscape. Official events see a real-life bagpiper welcome guests, while a recording will do at smaller dinners. 'The Selkirk Grace', a grateful epitaph to what will be eaten, comes next. Delivered by an elected chair, more commonly the most erudite pal at the table, its snappy riposte acknowledges those who go hungry at times of plenty:

> Some hae meat and canna eat,
> And some wad eat that want it,
> But we hae meat and we can eat,
> And sae the Lord be thankit.

The main attraction of a Burns supper is the infamous lump of bound offal or its vegetarian equivalent. Not only will the haggis be the focus of the meal, it too demands to be piped in, addressed with Burns' poem 'To a Haggis' and, finally, toasted by the guests. Typically, guests will then tuck into haggis, neeps (turnips) and tatties (mashed potato), with beer, single malt and water to accompany their meal. A variety of after-dinner speeches then follows, including a 'Toast to the Lassies', and the chance for female guests to reply with a witty retort.

There are all kinds of interpretations of Burns Night these days. Scottish brewers Innis & Gunn have previously teamed up with Macsween Haggis to host an afternoon in celebration of our national dish, where menus listed haggis-spiced chocolate and haggis Scotch eggs, while Glasgow comedy institution The Stand delivered a Burns-themed roll call of funny men including Scott Agnew and Vladimir McTavish who added some of the poet's best known lines into their acts. One past event, This Is Not A Burns Night, even provided a refreshing change for those in need of a break from Rabbie's verse.

Whether fans of his work or not, guests at a Burns Night should interact with one another in the spirit of lively debate rather than sit impassively. The key to hosting a coorie Burns evening is movement: linguistic and physical. Whisky plays a vital role, as it does in so many Scottish traditions.

The first time I ever threw a Burns supper party my haggis was cold and my mash lumpy, but everyone seemed in high spirits. Then I noticed that the two bottles of Highland Park I had bought for the table were empty before I'd even brought out the cranachan for dessert from the fridge.

Not one of my friends left on steady legs later that night. If they had, I'd have failed in my duty as a host.

A BURNS SUPPER FOR MODERN TIMES

Barry Bryson, private chef

Every year I'll cook at least four Burns suppers, for events ranging from street parties to corporate law firm dinners. The one thing I can never stray from is haggis. You can have Christmas without turkey, but Burns without haggis? Just no.

I know a lot of people like soft, wet food – it's very comforting – but I also like texture. So consider taking your Burns supper vegetables and griddling them instead. This gives the dish more architecture. I like the potato to be creamed (it's a bit weird to eat boiled potatoes with a Burns supper) to keep the same level of comfort food. As a dark food haggis doesn't photograph well, so varying the look of the plate is good for pictures.

On the subject of haggis, everyone has their favourite. Mine is from Shaw's Fine Meats, a butchers in Lauder, the Borders. I never have to adjust the seasoning. And the moisture content is just right for haggis canapés. For veggies, Macsween vegetarian haggis is nice and peppery.

Remove the external plastic then wrap the haggis in its sheath in foil and submerge in a bain-marie within a stockpot. Keep the temperature even, neither bubbling nor too slow. Too hot and your sheath will split. Cut the haggis into rounds like black pudding, pan fry it and turn it with a paddle slice as if you were frying fish.

Serve with a veal jus made from roasted veal bones cooked in stock, which is reduced, strained, returned to the pan and something sweet added such as honey or redcurrant jam. Cook down to a third.

You can finish off the dish with a drizzle of the jus on top. It looks wonderful with the orange of the swede and the whiteness of the potato. c

Now playing

Camera Obscura – 'Happy New Year'

Wild Coorie 6

In Scotland, the journey to a remote destination is part of the experience. Reaching the Rest and Be Thankful pass means you've come as far as the Cobbler, one of the southern Highlands' craggiest peaks. Drive from the south and see how the mountains begin to grow higher and knit together as you ascend, allowing only a sliver of road on the valley floor to dissect them.

In our most rural locations, extraordinary projects start as conundrums. In the case of Inver, a lochside restaurant set in Strachur, Argyll and Bute, owners Pam Brunton and Rob Latimer grasped a unique opportunity to put their mark on this waterlogged fringe of western Scotland.

Their Scandi-meets-Scottish restaurant feels imbued with calm as soon as you walk through the door. Harris Tweed upholstered seating flanks the windows and posies of wild grasses bring the outside in. But the road to Inver is the kind that creates friction between passenger and driver. Did you miss a junction or a turn? Whose job was it to watch out for the sign? Then a wooden board bearing the restaurant's name appears to mark your journey's end.

AT THE LOCHSIDE

When the couple took over in 2014 they found a 300-year-old fisherman's cottage in acute need of renovation. But one thing it didn't lack was character. The area they now call the Boatshed once formed a resting place for a vessel belonging to the cottage's former owner – a man who paid half his rent in the form of herring. Brunton and Latimer didn't feel the need to radically change the bones of the space. Today a wall of well-thumbed cookbooks in the Boatshed coexists with tasteful white walls built with thick stone to keep out the cold.

It's as if the landscape is
designed to facilitate discovery.

The cooking also avoids fuss, but that's not to say it is boring. Dining here is as much about the setting, looking out to the ruined Castle Lachlan, as the food. Broths and curious butters leave the kitchen, followed by great warming bowls of mutton. Plates are decorated with greenery as delicate as lightbulb filaments. They've got a great Scottish beer selection, too.

As a punter, you daren't think about how much work has gone into the logistics at Inver. Intelligent ingredients journey through rural Scotland, from Strathaven, Gigha and Ardkinglas, to reach the kitchen and become your dinner. It's a place that fizzes with smart thinking, and the front and back of house staff make the experience feel so smooth. The owners have polished and finessed just the right amount. As a result, a three-ingredient lochside supper is elevated into an artful creature.

INSHRIACH: AN ESTATE LIKE NO OTHER

Apparent simplicity best exemplifies coorie in the countryside. If we think a little harder about the effort places such as Inver take to run we know that to call them simple is to undermine the graft put in. Isolate the few component parts that come together to make the experience special and we can see they are the same threads that weave through the Scottish identity.

At Inver they are water, views and food. At Inshriach, a two-hundred-acre estate just outside of Aviemore, they are forests, self-sufficiency and invention.

Manager Walter Micklethwait has breathed new life into a curious range of buildings cobbled together on the cheap. I first met Walter in the summer of 2013, when I came to stay at

"Growing up in the late 1970s, coorie at my gran's house meant to keep warm and cuddle in. No double glazing or duvets then."

the Inshriach Bothy and write about it for an interiors magazine. The place bewitched me. You could spend weeks here, I realised, and it still wouldn't feel long enough. It was a Narnia moment: the door opening to a place that felt like an adventure playground for adults.

Central to Inshriach's success is its gin bar and farm shop, which won Channel 4's Shed of the Year award in 2015. It was built with signage from the UK's highest and smallest railway station in Dalnaspidal, and it is where Inshriach Gin is made from juniper berries and rosehips harvested from the estate.

In many ways Inshriach sums up what coorie is all about. Every year, Walter, his partner Lizzy Westman, and his mum, Lucy, welcome new residents to the Dog Shed, a small cottage that can be rented on a six-month basis by people from all kinds of backgrounds looking to ingrain themselves in the estate's way of life. For those open to meeting new folk and sharing ideas, Inshriach is a coorie haven. Those who come to spend a weekend alone can find peacefulness in the sauna, made with wood from an old horsebox, or the riverside hot tub.

The Beer Moth, a converted 1950s fire truck,

has salvaged Victorian floorboards laid to insulate the space, plus an astoundingly comfortable wrought-iron double bed. Log-burning stoves roar away in the yurt and shepherd's hut. Pull open the door, tip your head back and watch for shooting stars on an August night.

The bothy, arguably the slickest unit on site, is one of three around Scotland conceived by the artist Bobby Niven and the architect Iain Macleod as retreats. They are rented to artists, writers and makers on a residency basis, with the caveat that work produced must be in some way informed by Scotland. The original idea has grown legs: the initiative has since launched the Artist Bothy, a prefabricated structure for the consumer market. Anyone can stay at one of the existing bothies, then buy one of their own when they leave if they have the cash. Prices start from £39,000 – funds raised are ploughed back into the scheme.

TOOLS FOR LIFE AT CHIPPENDALE

Consumerism in Scotland has seen an interesting trajectory over the past decade. A return to traditional techniques – often the simplest solutions that haven't changed in more than two hundred years – has seen droves of students from around the world enrol at the Chippendale International Furniture School, a not-for-profit organisation nestled in a rural location on the outskirts of Gifford in East Lothian.

Founded in 1985 by Anselm Fraser, the school's workshops teach practical furniture-making skills and business acumen. Machinery dates from the 1920s to the current day.

The presence of Shellac, the studio tortoise, reminds everyone at Chippendale to take it slow.

When students arrive at the school they are often fresh from dry office jobs. Tired of working in a corporate setting, they want to learn how to be useful with their hands and make products built to last. Wood sourced by Anselm and his team comes from sustainable Scottish forests and is air dried outside for two years in a process known as "seasoning", before ending up in a kiln for a shorter burst of intense heat. Deviate from that method and the wooden furniture will break or warp easily after production.

At the end of each school year, all students leave with the knowledge of how to build a kitchen or a shepherd's hut. They will also have constructed three pieces of occasional furniture under the watchful gaze of tutors. Customers are responding – visitors to the school's biannual shows have reached record numbers in recent years as the trend for bespoke pieces continues.

Waking up in a hut like the kind Chippendale graduates are taught to make clarifies our relationship to the land around us. The things we think are essential to living melt away and less complicated ideas take their place. All we really need is fire, a place to wash, a desk to draw, or form, or think. Somewhere to capture a new view of the world and somewhere comfortable to sleep.

THE BEAUTY OF THE BOTHY

The current generation of huts might help creative folk focus on making new work, but the bothy's original function was more egalitarian. When the Mountain Bothies Association was founded in 1965, its plan was clear. It wanted to offer shelter in remote Scottish locations for walkers and climbers, the idea being that if hikers made the sacrifice to explore extreme locations they should be rewarded by basic accommodation that was free of charge. The concept was rolled out across the country and aroused a new kind of generosity among landowners. Only one of the association's bothies is actually owned by the organisation. More than a hundred of these shelters are provided by estate owners on the proviso they are left clean and undamaged.

"Bothying" came about as agricultural methods changed and farmsteads were increasingly abandoned. During the 1940s the idea of leisure was shifting as it began to mean roaming in the hills and countryside. Walkers looked for shelter on their meanderings, and these small buildings did the trick.

For a small annual fee, the association cares for the bothies in its charge and establishes new acquisitions. Most are one-room buildings made with local stone and corrugated tin roofs equipped only with an open hearth, plus rudimentary bunks. Others have little more than a stone floor and walls. All share the same unique highlight: they are sited within some of the most breathtaking scenery that rural Scotland has to offer. To come across a bothy is the closest experience Scotland has to a palm tree-dotted island mirage after hours stranded out at sea. With one slight difference: this vision is real.

The Schoolhouse, a corrugated tin bothy painted blue and grey set in an Easter Ross glen, was once a place of learning for the sons and daughters of ghillies who would tramp across land and loch to reach it, using stilts in high water. Rather than erase this slice of Scottish history, the association has kept it preserved. Campers looking for a coorie nook will still find blackboards and desks inside.

EARLSHALL CASTLE, THE ULTIMATE GRAND DESIGN

To me, one of the highlights of exploring the Scottish wilderness is spotting buildings that punctuate the landscape. They can be as humble as a doocot, as intriguing as an abandoned farmstead or as imposing as a ruined Palladian mansion. Each one will give clues to the people who have lived on and worked the land.

One of the most salubrious countryside buildings is Earlshall Castle, an astonishing private home in Fife.

Built in 1546, this Z-plan towerhouse in Leuchars, just outside of St Andrews, had fallen into disrepair by the late nineteenth century when it was abandoned and left to rot. However, its restoration in 1890 came as a turning point in pre-Industrial Revolution architecture. At the time it was unheard of to save old homes, the preferred option being to rip them down and start again. But conservators recognised Earlshall's faded beauty and pledged to fix her up.

Sir Robert Lorimer, then a fledgling architect, was tasked with the grand redesign. Earlshall's then owner, Robert Mackenzie, had faith Lorimer could make the towerhouse feel more liveable and, despite the young man's inexperience, he was right.

To add intimacy the architect commissioned a carved oak screen to split up the great hall, which had historically been loaned to townsfolk as a courtroom to settle disputes. A charming wooden summerhouse went into the grounds where yew trees trimmed into what the modern eye might see as giant green Daleks also stand.

What to one topiarist was junk, Lorimer saved and nurtured into horticultural heirlooms.

They were saved from a disused Edinburgh garden and brought to Earlshall in the 1890s.

Earlshall is now considered the residence that projected Lorimer into the league of super-architects. Thanks to one person's belief in young talent, a career was launched and a historic Scottish building saved. The present owners, Paul and Josine Veenhuijzen, open their gates to the public twice a year through the charity initiative Scotland's Gardens; locals from the village of Leuchars come for a nose about and tips are shared about what works best in the soil. The local church sometimes hosts barbecues and other community events in the grounds.

While the couple visit their homeland of Holland a few times a year, it is Scotland where they feel most at home. "Part of that is recognising something in Scotland that is stronger," says Josine. c

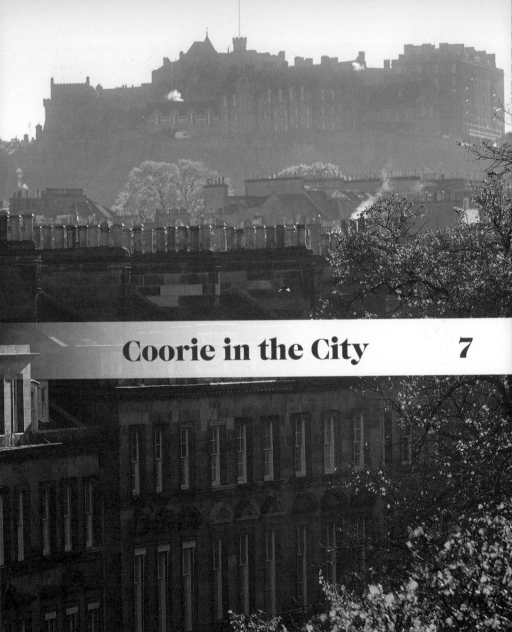

Coorie in the City 7

It's easy to think of coorie as an exclusively country pursuit. City neighbourhoods are governed by factors that challenge the principles of coorie, such as restrictions on log-burning stoves and planning bodies putting their foot down when it comes to leftfield ideas. Yet this hasn't diminished the aspirations of urban Scots determined to create and savour coorie in the best ways they can.

What's striking about the city as a construct is how it functions as a prism through which we contemplate our own identity and goals. The pubs or places of worship we spend time in reflect our own internal architecture, and one person's lived experience of a city can wildly oppose the next's. This makes conversations about coorie in the city all the more interesting.

In *The Prime of Miss Jean Brodie*, the beloved coming-of-age novel, Muriel Spark describes Sandy's shock after "speaking to people whose childhood had been [spent] in Edinburgh". The girl is amazed to discover "that there were other people's Edinburgh quite different from hers, and with which she held only the names of districts and streets and monuments in common".

The Edinburgh belonging to Jean Brodie's four young charges is a familiar backdrop against which they navigate the quicksand between youth and adulthood. The city's presence in the novel is its silent sixth character, in some ways the most distinctive, yet always a different friend to each of the girls. The city springs from the pages of the book thanks to Spark's passages on the Old Town in the 1930s and the sly politics of school life.

Your nose wrinkles in disgust at the miasma of squalid closes, but the city is also shown to transform its negative aspects to good. We read how "dark heavy Edinburgh itself could suddenly be changed into a floating city when the light was a special pearly white and fell upon one of the gracefully fashioned streets".

Coorie streets full of bustle might not always be beautiful, but there is always the potential to polish what is there. Parts of Edinburgh's formerly maligned districts have been buffed up in this way; they are now among the cooriest in the city.

Leith and the Shore are home to creative start-ups and Michelin-starred restaurants in converted warehouses that once stored grain and other industrial miscellany. One of the most exciting new openings for Leithers in recent years has been the Pitt Market, a trendy street-food hub open at the weekend. Come nightfall it's hard to spot friends through the billows of delicious-smelling smoke emitted from vendors' stalls, the scene illuminated with neon signs. It's not super expensive food, but it's still somewhere you save for a treat. Braving the chill for an alfresco supper is an act of sacrifice for a later pay off. The reward comes in a cardboard carton: Perthshire pheasant bao buns with cucumber and shaved green onions eaten around a brazier.

> "I remember being coorie at my gran's house next to her and my granda on the sofa, but now it's something I like to do with my dog."

Life in a Scottish city can feel like a constant grapple between what's best for us and what we desire. There are few finer sights than morning sunlight on sandstone tenements, but the reality of communal living means noise and neighbourhood tension are never too far away.

GLASGOW, A DEAR GREEN PLACE

When the Glasgow cityscape we know today was laid out in the mid nineteenth century, workers were housed in tall rows of flats, most in squalid conditions. Residents had communal 'back courts' instead of gardens, where bins and other assorted rubbish would be kept on a concrete courtyard and where washing would be hung out to dry. The majority of tenements have since been renovated or razed; the former option has created high-ceilinged private homes, while the latter paved the way for tottering new-build towerblocks springing from

the earth in places such as the Gorbals, many of which have now, in turn, been demolished. The lack of private outside space still endures for many Glaswegians, but at the city's famous second-hand market, the Barras, a green revolution promises to offset that.

A NATURAL HAVEN

Tuck Studio is a one-stop shop for botanical decoration. Part plant rehabilitation clinic, part succulent store and a space for independent artists and makers to sell their wares, it acts as a natural haven in this built-up corner of Glasgow. Sustainable living is at the heart of founder Tavienne Holley's vision. Her intention is to soften the sharp corners of our homes with thistles, brassicas, gypsy mist and eucalyptus, all grown organically and harvested in ways that don't cost the earth.

Tuck's founders sell greenery through

weekend markets held in the city, during which they also impart advice to growers keen to learn the rudimentary elements involved in keeping plants alive. Some of the potted plants you find in the shop may once have been abandoned in a garden centre bin and later nursed back to life by one of the staff. No shrub is a lost cause for the creative minds at Tuck, as they continue to offer tenement dwellers the next best alternative to a garden of their own.

TEA FOR ALL AT TCHAI-OVNA

A second stand-alone business in Glasgow shows how creative thinking can get an unlikely venture off the ground. Brothers Robin and Martin Fell and their friend Kenneth Shand opened Tchai-Ovna in 2000; the Fells pooled their student loans while in their second year at the University of Glasgow in order to start the tea house, which is a nod to their Czech-Scottish ancestry. From their coorie cave they now serve more than a hundred flavoured teas.

There's really nothing else like Tchai-Ovna in the city. Fairy lights frame the walls, cushions are mashed down into the grooves of the seats and the owners' cat stalks the floor space.

Orange Juice – 'Falling and Laughing'

While other cafés might have tweaked their menus from traditional Scottish breakfasts to smashed avocado on sourdough, Tchai-Ovna has carried on serving up cups of its famous Yogi Yogi Chai Masala. As a result, a destination tea room has been created, one that's comfortable in its own skin. For the most relaxed customers there's even a large bed at one side to coorie into.

Tchai-Ovna's location on Glasgow's Otago Lane has brought challenges of its own. Residents and business owners are fighting to keep the street's distinctive bohemian feel after planning permission was granted for a developer to build flats. They want the area to retain a diverse blend of people and to resist the council's obsession with profit.

FINDING COMFORT IN THE URBAN SPRAWL

Development does not have to mean rubbing out a past life. Take the brick and whitewashed pubs of Ashton Lane – a ten-minute walk from Tchai-Ovna – which started as factories and stables. What is now Bar Brel, a Belgian-inspired mussel house, was originally built as a coach house and garage to store a dark green Wolseley belonging to Dr Marion Gilchrist, who in 1894 was Scotland's first female medicine alumnus. The contemporary patrons of Ashton Lane come from the same families who have always drunk here.

The villages of diminutive buildings on Ashton and Ruthven Lanes act like ecosystems within Glasgow's wider environment. They offer a coorie rurality in an urban setting that helps us feel protected. Our cities might not be able to compete with the countryside for natural beauty, but they've created their own kind of visual interest that acts as a foil. If we look up as we wander through Old Aberdeen or Perth's Marshall Place the city will reveal its hidden parts.

THE PARLOUR OF DUNDEE

At Dundee's Westport, a street close to the River Tay, indie businesses act as a time machine. Westport has hosted local entrepreneurs as far back as the nineteenth century, when street numbers five to seven were Joseph Hynd's West End Clothing Company, and nine was owned by William Mather, a baker who opened his premises to the public as a "refreshment room".

These days, refreshment comes in the form of orzo salads and wedges of frittata served up in The Parlour, at number fifty-eight. This café's steamy windows are easily identifiable from half way down the road as the sun begins to set and its interiors glow through the gloom.

Owner Gillian Veal studied fine art at Duncan of Jordanstone College of Art and Design. After

travelling around India she returned to her native city to launch a café that allowed her to promote her love of contemporary vegetarian cooking and the food that comes fresh from the earth.

"I have a love of allotments and we have loads of them in Dundee," she says. "My whole degree show at art school was based around them, and I get great ideas from walking round seeing what the passionate growers are doing.

"I knew there was a need for a more modern café in Dundee but I had £4,000 and that was it. I couldn't afford a chef so I started cooking myself. As a lifelong veggie I cooked what I knew. Luckily for me people liked it."

Veal's customer base has swollen over the years to include transient diners popping in from the universities and local offices, but it is the people who first trudged through the doors in the early days who have become her adopted family.

"The Parlour is all about sharing our love and passion for food in an unpretentious way," she explains. "We still have the same customers fifteen years after opening: they held my babies while I got lunch ready, and I have employed some of their kids."

THROUGH THE LOOKING GLASS AT SPEX PISTOLS

It's serendipitous that The Parlour overlooks another of Dundee's cooriest shops. Spex Pistols' location is well concealed, but this hidden spot offers gains for the intrepid explorer. The retro-inspired optician's shop lies at the top of a winding lane and is famed for its instantly recognisable wall frieze depicting a 1950s maven in cat-eye frames. Spex Pistols is a shape-shifter: part treasure cabinet, part medical hub, and home to one of the oddest gadgets you'll find in the city.

On the back wall lives an "age-guessing" mirror developed by product designers from Dundee and Northumbria universities. The Self Reflector scans the face of the person looking into it and, through integrated speakers, plays a song from the year in which it deduces they turned fourteen. Spex Pistols' owners have described the oddity as the "best kept secret in Dundee", but a steady stream of curious visitors suggests wider knowledge of its existence.

THE BOOKSHOP AS A DISTRACTION

Coorie city places encourage new experiences. Their confines allow us to connect with our friends amid a mass of people passing in and out of the city limits. Every Scottish city is a product of the people who live in it and how each resident chooses to express themselves. Its coorie spaces offer distraction from the everyday drudgery of life.

Where better, then, to bring all these strands together than in the city bookshop? Bookshops of the world reflect the streets around the spot they inhabit: the nostalgic exoticism of Shakespeare and Company in Paris or San Francisco's offbeat Alley Cat Books. How better to typify Notting Hill in the film of the same title than William Thacker's charmingly chaotic bookshop, where the character agonises over his bumbling ineptitude with Anna Scott against a backdrop of travel guides useful only for lighting fires?

Scotland's bookshops are no different in the insight they provide. In Edinburgh, the shelves of Lighthouse Books are lined with titles leaking

ARMCHAIR BOOKS BOOKS

VICTORIAN
ILLUSTRATED
& SECONDHAND
BOOKS

CORDINER'S LAND

radical thought. Formerly known as Word Power Books, it was opened in 1994 by the author James Kelman and owned for twenty-two years by Elaine Henry, who also set up an imprint publishing short stories and anthologies written by women.

Now owned by Mairi C. Oliver, Lighthouse Books also spearheads magnanimous causes. It has hosted a sleepover to raise money for the city's homeless community, and the shop's basement is home to Streetreads, a charitable organisation that gives away books to the homeless. The charity's manifesto is that "a book is a place of escape and solace in a hard world". It's one I think we can all relate to.

If Lighthouse Books adds character to the central belt literary scene, Leakey's, in Inverness, is doing the same in the Highlands. This converted Gaelic church piles them high and plenty – second-hand books sprout beanstalk-like in stacks up to the mezzanine level, which doubles as an art gallery. At Leakey's heart is an enormous stove, kicking out heat from its enclosed pen. A wooden pulpit is the final resting place for the books staff keep behind the counter.

Don't expect to find order in the aisles of this northern star. But those who come to lose themselves in the musty romance of a second-hand bookshop can forget their worries for a few hours as they pore over unexpected gems found on the shelves.

No matter why we find ourselves in a city, human needs will always shine through. We all seek time with other people and by ourselves. Places to go to learn and be inspired. To find coorie reference points we just need to look with fresh eyes at the same streets we've walked down hundreds of times. Once we've learned to recognise coorie hallmarks, the only map we need is ourselves. c

Coorie Camping   8

All hail outdoorsy types. Where would we be without them encouraging us up mountains or wheedling until we cave in and head into the wilderness with a sleeping bag on our back?

Camping – and its chi-chi cousin, glamping – lends itself perfectly to coorie. Scotland's legal framework does, too: unlike England and Wales, where walkers must stay within set boundaries of the countryside, we can wander at whim. The same rights apply to sleeping overnight, which makes wild camping one of the most treasured aspects to roaming in Scotland. Hikers are safe in the knowledge that as long as they have a sensible tent and respect their surroundings, there is nothing to limit them. Come nightfall the adventure is far from over. In fact, a new one has just begun.

THE SMALL PRINT

Before you begin your coorie camping experience, take heed of the small print.

Because of floods of visitors to rural areas around Loch Lomond, in Argyll, a bylaw has been introduced to limit the number of campers. In order to maintain the area's natural beauty, campers must apply for a permit to stay between March and September in places that become especially busy.

The only other restriction applied to wild camping in Scotland is that an area is left as it is found. The Scottish Outdoor Access Code sets out guidelines on how best to interact with the environment to get the most from it. It recommends staying away from overcrowded spots so as to protect the land, and prohibits cutting down or damaging trees. All litter must be disposed of upon departure and campfires, while allowed, should leave no trace.

Some recommend lighting campfires on sand or stones, such as riverbanks and beds, to avoid the risk of grass scorch. If grass is the only option, online tutorials show how to avoid damage.

THE COORDINATES

After acknowledging the rules of the land, plan your route and overnight camping spot. In my opinion, the best resource detailing locations in which to camp is *Wild Guide Scotland*, a book with stunning imagery and helpful instructions on how to access places by foot. Among dozens of recommendations, the Quiraing landslip on the Isle of Skye is tipped by the authors; it's a

place where campers can watch dawn break "over spectacular plateaux". Glen Sannox, on the Isle of Arran, where waterfalls frame the forest, and the Lost Valley, in Glen Coe, with its name straight out of an Indiana Jones film, are also worthy inclusions. Those with calves that could crack walnuts should bike up the Bealach na Bà road, full of hairpin bends and set at an insane gradient, to get to Applecross campsite in Wester Ross. The rest of the group should follow in a car laden with the essentials.

It's worth pointing out that *The Art of Coorie*'s camping kit assumes a vehicle is involved, from which campers can make a short journey on foot to the site. You may have to sacrifice the chance to head into properly wild locations for these

cosy camping accessories, but feel free to edit the list as you see fit. You'll see that it offers ideas to make the experience more stylish, because who says camping has to be damp and utilitarian? Many of us have enough undesirable memories of camping as kids for that.

Overall, the idea is to set up a good-looking camp but avoid the kind of stressful walk from car to tent that can destroy friendships at fifty yards.

The list is by no means exhaustive but I hope it provides a starting point to which you can add your own bits and pieces. It also assumes you know to pack the boring stuff, such as a roll mat, extra-long matches and duct tape, plus all the food and drink you'll need for a feast.

COORIE CAMPING KIT

A great quality, lightweight backpack. It makes all the difference to the car-to-site walk of doom.

Two or three small-ish cushions. Thinner varieties of differing shapes can be layered and also squashed down and stored. Mix and match covers to suit. I like cushions in linen, herringbone and a patterned print, all in the same colour to avoid the look becoming OTT.

A sheepskin. This can be rolled up and threaded through a backpack's straps for convenience.

Cutlery and enamelware. Splatterware is seeing a return to form. Falcon enamelware, with its distinctive white and navy rimmed mugs and plates, is classic camping kit.

Ice cool box. This acts as a portable fridge for coorie cocktail ingredients. Place a rock or log on the lid to deter night-time creatures.

Light sources. Hanging a tea light lantern from the top middle point of tents creates a visual reference point in the dark. Use battery-operated tea lights to avoid the risk of your tent melting.

Stove and griddle pan. Everything tastes better cooked on a griddle. It's a fact of life.

In the daytime, set to work creating your coorie camp. At night, it's time to appreciate it. Technology has little place in coorie camping: this is a chance to chat properly, about ourselves, the universe and everything in between. A bottle of whisky may give way to the suggestion of skinny-dipping. I hear that's fun.

THE BOONS OF COORIE CAMPING

Coorie camping is about leaving your expensive devices at home and feeling like a wildling for the weekend. It's about taking turns to fetch water, boiling it and doling out cups of tea. What feels like a chore at home becomes fun on a camping trip. Decorate your tent with forest treasures until it looks like a woodland grotto, and share memory games played in childhood with adult friends. There is also the chance to get really good at making campfires. Fire is our oldest and most enduring form of heat and energy. Is it any wonder it's so important to our coorie experience?

Coorie camping gives life to experimentation. Recipes cobbled together with what's left in our packs are part of the fun. Have you ever eaten a griddled cheese toastie in the woods for breakfast? The excitement is in the preparation; someone firing up the kettle for a round of coffees, someone else getting the table (an upturned log) ready while the chef eases the sandwiches over, molten goo seeping from the sides and filling the air with the smell of roasted cheese. The radio might be on low, but more likely everyone is waking up slowly, listening to the sounds of the woods and working together to create a greater good. It's not what you'd eat at home. Any sense of a schedule is left behind and the experience is richer for it.

Told you a griddle pan was the key to happiness. ᴄ

Now playing

Arab Strap – 'Loch Leven'

COORIE TIP: For a cosy light source
guaranteed to withstand rain, buy battery
operated fairy lights or frosted mini bulb
string lights. Wind them around your hand
until they're tightly coiled then wedge
into a mason jar before sealing the lid
shut. The result is a waterproof lamp
worthy of a fairy glen.

FIVE OF THE BEST STARGAZING SPOTS IN SCOTLAND

Borve, Isle of Harris

The west coasts of Harris and Lewis offer wild scenery, white sandy beaches and – in winter – there's barely a soul to be seen. Try Horgabost campsite, located a short drive from Luskentyre beach overlooking the island of Taransay, where the UK's first reality TV show, *Castaway*, was filmed. Allow your eyes thirty minutes to adjust to the darkness and look out for Polaris.

Isle of Coll

A designated Dark Sky Island, Coll has no street lights. Here, the chance of seeing the Aurora Borealis is about as good as it gets on Scotland's west coast. Three locations have been allocated for dark sky viewing, including the RSPB nature reserve at Totranold, but chances of seeing the Milky Way's brightest band are good all over. Coll's high number of bright, sunny days also adds to its chances of clear, moonlit nights.

Galloway Forest Park, Dumfries & Galloway

Said to be home to the darkest sky in the whole of Europe, Scotland's largest forest is located about seventy miles from the nearest city. The Scottish Dark Sky Observatory, in Dalmellington, has a retracting roof to make it easier to see constellations, while two powerful telescopes help visitors track stars. The Andromeda Galaxy and stellar nurseries, where new suns of distant planets are born, can also be spotted.

Edinburgh

Urban locations are never going to match rural parks when it comes to star watching. But for nights when it's not viable to venture out of the city, Edinburgh's Royal Observatory on the grassy slopes of Blackford Hill is the place to be. If the observatory's Victorian telescope dome isn't impressive enough, the meteorites passed around are bound to amaze. Weather permitting, stargazing is undertaken outside on the observatory's flat roof.

Glenuig, Lochaber

Most of the Highlands fare well in the stargazing stakes, but campsites in the Lochaber area are treated to particularly beautiful skies. Glenuig, a small village thirty-five miles west of Fort William, is close to the dramatic tidal island of Eilean Shona, where wild campers stay over on grassy outcrops of land. Golden eagles soar through the skies during the day, but when the sun dips below the waterline it's time to coorie down for nature's luminous attractions. c

The Coorie Pub 9

Is there any other place where a more vibrant palette of human behaviour can be observed than the Scottish pub?

Our drinking holes are social spaces, shelters and, with the rise of flexible working and free WiFi, informal offices. The pub is a courtroom, a therapist's clinic, a place to let socks dry out after an arduous day orienteering. Relationships begin and end in its confines. Pub dogs become celebrities. Just ask Simba the Rhodesian Ridgeback, who frequents bars on Glasgow's Woodlands Road.

If we run with the myth that there are languages with fifty words for snow, Scots could match that with their own terms related to the act of drinking. If you're hoolit, buckled, blazin' or steamin', you've had one too many. The next morning your heid might be birlin' and sair, you'd be hangin', rough or due for a spew. For some, the only cure is to "get back on it".

HISTORY OF THE HANGOVER

In James Boswell's *The Journal of a Tour to the Hebrides*, the biographer laments a well-oiled night spent with his and Samuel Johnson's host. Although published in 1785, the passages on drinking show that the alcohol-related anxiety we know today as "the fear" is far from unique to our time.

After a night of debauchery on the Isle of Skye, Boswell writes:

I awakened at noon, with a severe head-ache ... I was much vexed that I should have been guilty of such a riot, and afraid of a reproof from Dr Johnson ...

Soon afterwards, Coirechatachan, Coll, and other friends assembled round my bed. Corrie had a brandy-bottle and a glass with him and insisted I should take a dram.

"Ay," said Dr Johnson, "fill him drunk again. Do it in the morning, that we may laugh at him all day. It is a poor thing for a fellow to get drunk at night, and skulk to bed, and let his friends have no sport."

Far from reprimanding his employee, Johnson finds Boswell's predicament a laugh. It shows that the hangover is a chance for men and women of any background to bond, a universal language that has survived the test of time like a relic.

THE ENDURING APPEAL OF THE PUB

Scots have sat to sip alcohol with friends for centuries. The coorie roadside coach houses with space to tether a horse may since have been upgraded into speakeasies with copper fittings, but the original idea endures. They are still a place to let thoughts uncoil after a tough day out in the world, where it is possible to be solitary and sociable at the same time.

As is the case in many countries around the world, numerous pubs purport to be the oldest in Scotland. These include the Sheep Heid Inn, in Duddingston, Edinburgh, where liquor has been sold on site since 1360.

One of my favourite Scottish terms – "to keep the heid", or to keep calm – is where Scots can go wrong in the pub. Don't be gripped with Boswell levels of fear the morning after drinking; instead, here are some of the cooriest pubs in which to drink in moderation.

THE DROVERS INN
Inverarnan, Argyll and Bute

Not every pub greets punters with a stuffed menagerie. The Drovers' collection of taxidermy has inspired countless selfies over the years, in particular the lobby's bear with his snarling teeth and put 'em up paws. Inside is a microcosm of Scotland: tartan upholstery, haggis, neeps and tatties on the menu, and even rumours of a ghost to keep overnight guests guessing about creaking floorboards. The inn's location explains its appeal further: it lies within Loch Lomond & The Trossachs National Park.

THE POT STILL
154 Hope Street, Glasgow

While Edinburgh's core bursts with atmospheric boozers that appear largely untouched by gentrification, the drinking dens of Glasgow city centre have been polished to within an inch of their lives. Look past the slick basement bars to the Pot Still, established in 1867 and where malts outnumber punters. The pub claims to have seven hundred whiskies behind its counter; bottles teeter in cabinets stacked up to the ceiling, threatening to fall on the heads of staff who edge them out tentatively like Jenga pieces.

THE TOURMALET
25 Buchanan Street, Edinburgh

Every neighbourhood needs a pub with a cornucopia of wall-mounted tat. Leith's is the Tourmalet. It manages to navigate the tricky ground between keeping long-term locals happy and appealing to the hipster crowd thanks to its broad selection of Scottish ales, knowledgeable bar staff and laid-back vibe. While drinking here one night I saw two drinkers have a Chinese takeaway delivered and sit happily munching away while the barman nodded over his approval. Any establishment happy to dispose of stuffy pub rules like that should be applauded.

Now playing

Gerry Cinnamon – 'Belter'

"Coorie is a favourite of my mum and grandparents who were Aberdonian, so I always think of them when I hear it."

HOOTENANNY
67 Church Street, Inverness

Any nocturnal adventure in Scotland's most northern city should begin or end in Hoots. Tardis-like, its capacious floor plan weaves around a central bar stocked to the brim with reasonably priced malts. Decor is well-considered: the walls are papered with pages torn from old issues of the *Northern Chronicle*, the long-gone local newspaper, while candles wedged in empty liquor bottles illuminate the silhouettes of drinkers like an Old Master painting. Music comes in the form of bagpipes emitted from the stereo, later swapped for live folk sessions.

THE OLD BRIDGE INN
23 Dalfaber Road, Aviemore

This pub, nestled in the Cairngorms National Park, has become a destination point for walkers and travellers who plan a trip specifically to end up here after a day in the hills. The Old Bridge Inn has few pretensions – its menus swerve stuffy fine dining thanks to easy, familiar ingredients – and beamed ceilings add true Highland character.

The back end of the inn is devoted to more casual drinking, centred on a log fire with bar stools and tables set close to each other, while the top is a more formal restaurant space.

THE SHIP INN
The Toft, Elie, Leven

Not all coastal pubs are created equal. The Ship Inn's success lies in its rejection of twee decor tropes associated with the seaside location. Instead of pastel wall prints, vintage oars give a minimalist nod to the setting, while wooden barrels make for informal tables. Those close to the windows have a vantage point over Elie beach and, as the sun sets behind the water, the shore is illuminated in pink and orange tones. Most of the options on the menu are gluten free, so coorie into one of the plaid-upholstered armchairs and order a bowl of soup before heading out on to the sand.

THE GLOBE INN
56 High Street, Dumfries

A tiny window with words by Robert Burns etched on to the glass hints at the Globe Inn's history. Built in 1610, its location down an inconspicuous alleyway on Dumfries High Street belies its cultural significance: Scotland's bard was a regular who came to sup ale during a stint living in the town. These days, the inn's stable has been converted into a lounge, while the main bar serves a Burns lager on tap. It also functions as a love letter to the wordsmith: written correspondence branded with the poet's insignia lies beside modern representations of his face on gifts in cabinets. **c**

Coorie Gardens 10

I'm certain that our friends from around the world find it hilarious that as soon as the sun makes an appearance we rush to sit out on our patios and balconies clutching hot drinks. "Isn't it lovely?" we tell each other, our voices barely audible through the chatter of our teeth.

Even in summer the Scottish weather can be so changeable that we have learned to adapt our gardens, putting up seagrass walls to shield lawns and installing barbecues in sunken courtyards in an attempt to prevent being driven inside by the wind.

Like our homes, a garden is an extension of taste and preference. It can be a hobby room, a zone for entertaining, a junkyard and a display of creativity. Somewhere to take a gulp of air or wine – whichever is the most necessary.

The garden also works hard. It is a place to hang washing, to store equipment, bikes and ladders, to hose down a muddy dog. Those of us with gardens big enough to execute our visions prove that projects can be born combining many of these elements, sometimes even all.

Coorie gardens all have a place

that encourages reflection

and peacefulness.

Coorie gardens have a common trait: there will be at least one place that encourages reflection and peacefulness. A coorie spot could be a garden grotto, blending into the scenery with trained climbers concealing its form, or a basic summerhouse with space to sit. A balcony with a comfortable chair where you can turn your face to the sun and read a book is a perfect coorie space. Even a shared back court with a picnic bench can be dressed with lanterns and potted plants to conjure the feeling of coorie. Some intrepid souls might like to string a hammock out to evoke the ultimate sense of downtime.

Gardeners with coorie on the brain don't have to look far for inspiration. An urban jungle can easily be created on a tiny city terrace, either with the help of experts or by swapping ideas with green-fingered friends.

Professional gardeners recommend looking around to see what context your outside space falls within to give you clues on design. If the spires of a large granite church or leaves of a copper beech tree can be seen close by, echo the colours and shapes.

However, rather than going for the DIY approach, rising numbers of Scots are taking the easy route and employing landscape designers. Their budgets aren't small, but there are takeaway tips we can glean from the work and imagination that landscapers have put into Scottish gardens.

EATS, SHOOTS AND LEAVES

To start, planters large enough to host quick-growing shrubbery work best on terraces, but think about how much light your outside space receives. Try foliage in shady spots and grasses in areas that are scorched by the wind. Once established, greenery should also provide an extra layer of shelter to protect you when you're sitting outside with a morning coffee.

Next, consider how you will feed your plants. Installing an outside water tap that feeds from the garden or kitchen costs less than £100 and avoids having to trail through your home with a watering can threatening to slop all over your floors. Light sources are the final, crucial addition to coorie gardens – as they are in most ideas relating to the concept. If your outside space has a pagoda or loggia, roof-hung lighting creates a beguiling grotto effect.

FULL GROTTO MODE: ACTIVATE

Coorie garden grottoes of all shapes and sizes have been around for thousands of years, originally built over sacred springs as places of worship in Greece. Over time they became something wealthy landowners wanted to have built for pleasure: a refuge in an expanse of garden where tea could be drunk alone or with company. Gentry spent years, even decades, perfecting their garden rooms with the help of architects.

Today's obsession with man caves and she sheds – and other non-gender-specific structures such as cabins, bothies and summerhouses – isn't all that surprising when we consider how far back our love affair with the grotto spans. Decorations for a garden grotto come in many styles, but one source of inspiration that has survived the years is the seashore.

The shell grotto has a rich and illustrious history in Scotland, with many eighteenth-century examples found in Cockenzie, Gosford and Newhailes.

These artificial caves have also inspired the coorie gardeners of today. A lifelong infatuation with the shell grotto led Lady Ann Fraser to consider commissioning one of her own in the grounds of Shepherd's House, a late seventeenth-century home in Inveresk, near Musselburgh, where she has lived with her husband, Charles, since 1957.

A HOUSE OF SHELLS

The German artist Albrecht Dürer's statement that "art is hidden in nature" could have been written about the Frasers' garden. It is a place where layers of colourful shrubs and flowers have evolved over more than half a century. The borders act as an earthy archive for specialist snowdrop varieties; more than seventy named types bloom throughout the winter.

In 2013, it was time to add a manmade curiosity to the collection. "Ever since childhood I have been fascinated by shells," says Lady Fraser. "A shell house has always been a dream, but it was only having seen the one at the Royal Botanic Garden Edinburgh created in memory of the Queen Mother that we decided to build our own."

The couple approached architect Lachlan Stewart to conceive their shell house. They wanted a grotto that reflected the story of their lives and brought in elements of their surroundings. Almost six months after building started, the bones of their shell house were in place. Then it was time for the fun part.

"Five art student friends of Lachlan's daughter arrived with boxes of scallops, limpets and mussels, and together we worked out a design," Lady Fraser recalls. "We had also collected shells with the family and there was no shortage of mussels and cockles on the beach at Musselburgh."

Each shell had to be attached to the walls with tile cement, a slow and considered process. In every corner of the shell house lies a detail chosen to bring the Frasers joy: the stained glass windows were created by the artist Amanda Mitchell and feature Lady Fraser's favourite flowers. Far from shutting out the world

around them, the Frasers chose to incorporate it into the design.

"The weather vane is a homage to a mallard duck that used to nest every year on top of the ivy-covered, tumbledown old shed, proudly hatching numerous ducklings," they say. "And the quote on the bench is by Charles Rennie Mackintosh. It reads: 'Art is the Flower – Life is the Green Leaf. Let every artist strive to make his flower a beautiful living thing, something that will convince the world that there may be, there are, things more precious more beautiful – more lasting than life itself.'"

"Art is the Flower.

Life is the Green Leaf."

A LIBRARY BOOK AND A RIVERBED

Another green-fingered Scot and his family have taken similar delight from the coorie structure in their grounds. John Irvine's Tikki Hut lies at the foot of his garden, in West Linton, the Borders, providing a visual break between the back of the house and the end of the green space.

"The idea was to create a focal point from the garden room that looks out over the garden," he says. "Although we have trees as a beautiful background, it needed something bigger than that in the foreground."

That "something bigger" is an octagonal summerhouse with a quaint thatched roof. It was built by John forty years ago, and remains a testament to what can be done with limited resources.

Having never thatched a roof before, John took out a book from the local library to teach himself how. His first job was to source the reeds with which to thatch the Tikki Hut's roof, which was constructed using rafters built up to a meeting point from the structure's wooden walls.

The roof was no easy feat for this amateur thatcher. "I had an awful job of sourcing the reeds but I eventually found them on the banks of the River Tay," John says. "Reed beds had been laid there a hundred years ago to grow what was used for packing materials before the days of polystyrene."

After locating a small firm that sold the reeds in bundles, and with the help of his library book, John spent three months over the summer of 1978 acquainting himself with the art of thatching.

"A garden breaks the cycle of thoughts."

It was "very much a case of trial and error" but he remained relaxed about learning. "You change your ideas as you go along – you have no choice but to," he explains.

Bundles of reeds were unrolled around the timber frame and held in place with iron hooks and hazel rods. Every year John goes round with a leggett – a blockheaded wooden paddle – and thumps the rows of reeds upwards to squash them back into place, since they have a tendency to succumb to gravity.

He also gives the walls, which are made of Western red cedar, an annual varnish. While he cannot remember exactly how much the building cost to construct, it was not an exercise in extravagance. "It could not have been too expensive because I am not a rich man," he says. "The reason I built it was because I could

not afford to buy a summerhouse at the time."

His hard work has rewarded him with a coorie space with remarkable sound and heat absorption. It is a spot where John and his late wife, Laura, sat during the summer to eat breakfast together in warm weather and one where he now enjoys a cup of tea to look out at nature's handiwork.

"I am not a horticulturist, but gardening is a super hobby to have," he says. "Your head is whizzing round with problems when you finish work and you are not in a good state of mind. But then you step outside.

"My wife would say: 'We're having dinner in an hour – go outside until then.' It worked. You go out and before you know it you have seen something that distracts you. It is the most wonderful therapy." c

Coorie Food and Drink   11

Cocteau Twins – 'Cherry Coloured Funk'

Pick up any book about Scottish food and drink and count the times you spot the phrase "Scotland's natural larder". It's a hackneyed term, but there's truth buried in the cliché.

It's easy to focus on the negative aspects of Scotland's cold, damp weather, but those same conditions give life to mountains of potatoes and more raspberries per capita than any other EU country.

Coorie dishes feature Scottish ingredients that keep us cheered and nourished. These recipes stand for more than just fuel. A steak pie on New Year's Day signifies hope for the months ahead. Gravy coagulating in cuts of steak is a liquid message of thanks for surviving the year just passed.

Foodie innovators are using Scottish herbs, berries and other edible gems in exciting new ways. The humble Scots pine needle is being bashed and bruised by chefs to add flavour to food, either as a dry cure or in cooking. Sourced from forests or back gardens, it's a really simple way to update flavour profiles. And, in most cases, it's free.

A second trend, veganism – and vegetarianism – is winning over sworn carnivores and proving the benefits of a meat-free lifestyle. This, in turn, appears to be recalibrating the output of chefs who were previously all about meat and fish. It's not hard to walk down West Port, in Dundee, or the West End, in Aberdeen, after dark these days and see plates of zingy courgette or kimchi-inspired cabbage flowing out of restaurant kitchens.

Coorie eating can be done alone. Coorie is there when we derive unbidden pleasure from scratching fork marks on the tattie topping of stovies for one while cooking at home or heading out by yourself for a bite to eat. Research by the bookings website 5pm shows that the number of diners booking a table for one at Scottish restaurants has risen sixfold in the last five years. Consumer experts tie

the trend to our contemporary predilection for smartphones. With them, solo diners do not feel alone.

Coorie eating with company is a different beast. One that's loud, sometimes raucous, involving long, drawn-out nights with a patchwork of dishes and mismatched glasses being clinked.

FRIENDS AND STRANGERS

In the early days of writing *The Art of Coorie* I headed north to a pal's place in pursuit of some headspace. The night I arrived I opened the kitchen door to his house and was greeted with the most delicious smell of dinner simmering on the hob, a stew made using pheasant shot from near the estate. The rough wooden table was packed with folk – friends of his but strangers to me – a Celtic musician and his girlfriend, another writer who had also come to work on a project, plus assorted family members.

The acts of divvying up roast potatoes, of ensuring sleeves didn't go up in flames when wafting over candles, and of making sure the baby was kept entertained meant that by the end of the meal a new level of camaraderie had been forged. What we ate played an important role in that feeling of togetherness. Food wasn't just there to fill us up. It was a conversation starter to block unsure silences and feel grateful for. Life doesn't get coorier than that.

TREASURE HUNTING IN THE FOREST

There's a childlike excitement that comes with heading out into the woods for mushrooms. It's the same feeling as you'd get from finding a shiny conker under a pile of leaves with your school friends. The best harvesters know a patch of land ripe with mushrooms and keep it a closely guarded secret. If they told you, they'd have to kill you.

My own chanterelle-picking pal lives on the Ardkinglas Estate, in Cairndow, a little over an hour west of Glasgow. Early one September morning we headed into the Argyll Forest to see what we could find – to my amazement these little orange fungi were sprouting everywhere. He showed me that the largest mushrooms aren't always the best – the younger, springier varieties are king of the woods. It proved to me that you really do need to know what you're doing when it comes to foraging, not only to select the best tasting fungi but also to make sure you don't end up consuming a species that's going to do you harm. We ended up picking enough to fit in two tubs and headed back to his cottage to fry them up in a pan with hot butter and parsley, then scranned the lot on the drive to work. Coorie breakfast heaven.

A COORIE DIET

Scotland has a bad reputation for its diet, and not one that's always deserved. From the way the world's press writes about the deep-fried Mars bar you'd think we were eating nothing else. The chippies of my hometown still sell the pizza crunch – a folded pizza dipped in batter and deep fried – but who are we to suggest that whoever enjoys them doesn't also eat kale, broccoli or bananas? A coorie diet should be varied and include all the ingredients that give us the gastro horn ... within reason. A dinner prepared by a Michelin-starred chef, a late-night takeaway box of chips and cheese, and a bowl of homemade cock-a-leekie soup aren't mutually exclusive meals.

Coorie cooking isn't the time to practise parsimony. In a world where the seemingly ubiquitous "clean eating" trend threatens to erase the culinary heritage of nations, coorie cooking flicks the V at cutting back and cutting out.

To cook with coorie in mind is about sequences, about messing up and starting again. Interviewing chefs in my day job always brings me equal amounts of pleasure and frustration: pleasure because their recipes make me salivate at my desk and frustration about their relaxed approach to measurements and time in the oven. "What temperature?" I ask. "Just as long as it needs," they reply.

So maybe we're too hung up on getting it right first time. There is joy to be found in a fatalistic attitude when cooking, in experimenting without fear of recrimination. But there's also joy in eating food that tastes good when we've limited time, finances or energy, so the following three tastemakers have included their methodology in the recipes below. Each features a classic Scottish ingredient or dish brought into modern times.

VSO HENDERSON
Head chef at The 78, formerly Harmonium and Mono

I'm trying to get more people into vegan food. Folk like my dad, Iain Henderson, a working-class painter and decorator from Clydebank who likes his meat and two veg for every meal. If he can come in to a vegan restaurant and enjoy it then anyone can.

That's why I want to do a vegan version of traditional Scottish food – the kind of food I grew up with. This Cullen Skink was the kind of thing we had when we couldn't afford a lot of ingredients so we made big pots of the stuff. It was always an exciting meal for me in our house.

People expect food of a certain standard these days, and as vegan chefs we need to give them it. Even if a vegan place isn't fine dining it should still meet those standards. I'm trying to take things back to simple, tasty food – not disguising the flavour of vegetables, grains and pulses. All they need is a bit of roasting or using other simple ways of seasoning to bring the taste out.

Vegan Cullen Skink with salsify crisps

For the salsify crisps
Method
1 Peel two salsify roots and with a mandoline shave crisps out of them. If you don't have a mandoline, thinly slice the roots, and if you can't find salsify then parsnip or any nice sweet root vegetables will do.

2 Shallow fry till golden, pop on a piece of kitchen towel and sprinkle with flaky sea salt.

For the Cullen Skink
Ingredients
- 50ml of oil
- 1 tbsp of vegan butter
- 1 large white onion, diced
- 2 garlic cloves, roughly chopped
- 1 medium leek, sliced into rounds
- 6 Maris Piper potatoes, peeled and

chopped into medium cubes
- 1 400g tin of jackfruit in brine (not syrup)
- 1 litre of soya milk (any plant-based milk will do but ones with higher fat content work better)
- 1 250ml carton of soya cream (again, can be any plant-based cream)
- 1 vegetable stock cube or two tbsp of Bouillon powder mixed with 1 litre of boiling water
- Juice of a lemon
- 4 tbsp of liquid smoke (you can buy this from most American or world food sections in supermarkets or online)
- Fresh chives
- Flaked sea salt and cracked black pepper

Method

1 Add the oil and butter into a heavy-based pot and bring the heat up to medium.

2 Add the onions and leek and sauté off until translucent.

3 Then add the potatoes and garlic, and once they have been coated with the oil and butter add some of the liquid stock until it is just covering the vegetables. Let this cook off gently as you want to soften up the potatoes enough before you add the rest of the liquids.

4 Add the jackfruit, the liquid smoke and a little bit more of the stock.

5 Keep cooking until both the potatoes and the jackfruit start to break up a little; you may want to gently nudge them with a wooden spoon. This helps the soup thicken up and gives it a creamy texture.

6 After about 10 to 15 minutes start to add the rest of the ingredients.

7 Add the soya milk and give it a stir, then add about a half of the carton of cream. If you want it richer, pour the whole carton in.

8 Let it cook off for another 10 minutes then add your seasoning and the juice of a lemon.

To serve

Give the Cullen Skink a wee taste; it can be altered if you like it smokier, saltier, maybe with more pepper.

I like mine quite salty and smoky as those are the flavours I remember from when my mum, Sheila, made me this when I was a wean, along with either a big chunk of crusty, buttery bread or rough oatcakes to mop it up.

When you are ready to serve, make sure it's up to temperature, portion up the soup into deep bowls so you can fit all those potatoes and jackfruit in there. Then garnish with the salsify crisps and some freshly chopped chives.

BEN READE AND SASHANA SOUZA ZANELLA

Founders, Edinburgh Food Studio

When we talk about Scottish cuisine being an expression of our culture, we first have to recognise that we don't have a single identity. It is a collage of different cultures that comes together.

This recipe came into existence when we hosted the Colombian chef Jaime Rodriguez at the Edinburgh Food Studio. One of the dishes he prepared was called Bollo di Pollo, or chicken balls.

One of the things we found exciting was that it was a technique we could apply to other dishes. It had a logic we can use within Scottish cuisine: we love birds, we love smoked food, and the peasemeal from Golspie Mill in Sutherland is a wonderful ingredient we should explore further.

The responsibility to do that lies with us as chefs.

Clootie Baws

For the glaze
Ingredients
- 1 onion
- 1 carrot
- 1 celery stick
- 2 cloves of black garlic
- 2 cloves of regular garlic
- Smoked guinea fowl bones
- 2 glasses of red wine
- Bay leaf
- Few sprigs of thyme

Method
Cook all ingredients for three hours in a pressure cooker, or simmer for five hours in a normal pot. Strain, skim and reduce into a glaze. Set aside.

For the filling
Ingredients
- One or two hot smoked guinea fowl or chicken breasts, shredded with fingers. Learn how to smoke meat in chapter 16.
- 1 onion
- 1 carrot
- 1 stick celery
- 1 garlic clove
- 2 cloves of black garlic
- Wild leek
- Sprig of thyme
- Glaze from above

Method
Sauté all the vegetables, then fold in the shredded meat, loosen with glaze, and adjust seasoning to taste. Set aside.

For the peasemeal pancake
Ingredients
- 300g peas (good frozen ones are fine)
- 100g peasemeal (a traditional yellow pea flour that you can buy online)
- 1 heaped tsp baking powder
- Up to 50ml hot stock
- 70g Crowdie soft cheese
- Salt to taste
- Parchment / greaseproof paper

To serve
You will need your foraging skills:
- Handful of wild garlic, sautéed
- Wild mushrooms, such as scarlet elf cups
- Ground elder shoots

1 Put ingredients in a bowl and add hot stock until you have a dough-like consistency. Allow to cool.

2 Take 60g of mixture and flatten between parchment paper with a heavy saucepan.

3 Discard paper, then take 35g of smoked meat mix and place in the middle of the pancake. Pull edges of the dough up to form a small purse. Remove bits where the dough is doubled up.

4 Pull a double layer of cling film up and around the peasemeal ball, and twist off the end, turning the pancake 'purse' into a tight ball. The ball can now be kept overnight or frozen until needed.

5 Steam the ball for 10 minutes until cooked. Then serve with the glaze, sautéed wild garlic, scarlet elf cups and ground elder shoots.

LYNSEY CAMERON
Head bartender, Bar Gandolfi

I've named this take on the hot toddy after a Doric term I was told. Hummel doddies is Doric for mittens, which I've tweaked to Humble Doddy. I thought it was both adorable and pretty fitting.

It starts with a measure of your favourite whisky. This is best suited to a sweeter Speyside or a lightly peated malt. My favourites are Jura, Oban 14, or Caol Ila for something with a bit more of a smoky kick.

There's no riddle to making a hot toddy and there are no hard and fast rules. It's what I'd call a "house drink". It's easy and it helps you use up ingredients you might have lying about – such as the malt miniatures you get for Christmas.

The berry reduction adds an extra element of colour and sweetness to the drink, which turns it into more of an event than the conventional hot toddy. Try making a batch of the reduction then freezing the leftover liquid into an ice tray. Just add a single cube to the hot toddy in the future.

Humble Doddy

For the berry reduction
Ingredients
- 100g frozen soft fruits such as brambles (blackberries), raspberries and blackcurrants
- Two slices of lemon
- Three cinnamon sticks
- 200ml water
- Sugar, to taste

1 Heat the berries with the lemon slices in water for about 20 minutes or until the skins of the blackcurrants burst and the brambles lose their colour.

2 Strain the fruit and heat for a further 5 to 10 minutes with the cinnamon sticks and add sugar to taste. The reduction can be kept in the fridge for around a week and will stay fresh and can be easily reheated.

For the Humble Doddy
Ingredients
- 50ml good whisky
- 50ml camomile tea
- Splash of berry reduction or one cube of frozen liquid

1 Add the whisky to the camomile tea and then some of your homemade berry reduction.

2 Add other herbs and spices, such as cloves, according to taste. c

Coorie Textiles 12

136 J ↑   145 J ↑   146 J ↑

Back when the internet was just a twinkle in Bill Gates' eye, the easiest way to show your colours was through what you wore. Clothing is a political beast: garments are born from cultural tribalism as much as they are necessity, and Scotland can more than hold its own in terms of a politically charged customer base.

The elements involved in textile production are found in abandon here, from water that powers mills, to enough sheep to knit socks for a woollen army. It's little wonder we've been churning out some of the world's most revered fabrics for five centuries or longer.

Scotland's textiles range wildly in pattern, texture and style, but all share a set of core credentials. Firstly, they must perform the job they were created to do, keeping the wearer cosy and dry. Historically, textiles were made by hand in such a way that ensured durability so they would not fall apart after a few wears. After all, these were the years before mass production, when the make do and mend attitude reigned supreme.

Yet even when loom and machine manufacturing came into play, our Scottish textiles were still known for their quality and craftsmanship. It might take our weavers longer to make garments, but the wait is always worth it.

BEGINNINGS OF NATIONAL DRESS

When it came to making cloth, Scots looked around them for where to begin. They saw wool – bags of it – sheared from the eleven varieties of native Scottish sheep. They dyed it using the roots of vegetation before drying, teasing and carding. Eventually it became thread and yarn that could be woven to create tartan, tweed, knitwear and lace.

You only have to run your hand over the dozens of kilts hanging in Armstrong's vintage shop, on Edinburgh's Grassmarket, to get an understanding of the skill involved in constructing each garment and wonder about its history. When you wear a pair of tweed trousers

or a tartan bow tie manufactured in Scotland you aren't simply making a fashion statement. It's a consumer choice that keeps our heritage alive and our workforce in employment. Established Scottish brands have seen an interesting trading journey over the past twenty years as fast fashion in the nineties and noughties changed the way people bought clothes.

In recent times, a return to "slow goods", where customers want to invest in a brand's back story, has seen their resurgence.

In 2014, the high street store Hobbs began buying lace from MYB Textiles, a mill in Ayrshire dating back to 1913, after one of their designers visited the factory on holiday. Fashionistas looking for limited edition designs have also

Harris Tweed production ran to about seven million metres of cloth in the 1960s, but had dropped to just 500,000 in 2009. By 2012, however, the Harris Tweed Industry Forum said it had seen its best year in fifteen years.

altered the output of cashmere specialist Johnstons of Elgin. "We're seeing consumer demands change," says David Hamilton, the company's director of operations. "We've been in business for over two hundred years and we're constantly asking ourselves what the next two hundred years will look like."

TARTAN

The first mentions of tartan occurred in the late sixteenth century, but it took another hundred years for this woven woollen fabric to be linked to particular families. By the mid eighteenth century it took on another role, as Highlanders banned from wearing the kilt following the Dress Act of 1746 began to don it as a rebellious snub to authorities' rule.

Our national dress was once so feared that it was illegal to wear tartan in Scotland. When the ban was repealed in 1782, overcoming this repression made us all the more hungry to keep tartan's place in our wardrobe.

What's fascinating about tartan is that versions of checked material have been discovered in ancient settlements all over the world. According to the textile historian E.J.W. Barber, the Hallstatt culture of Central Europe that flourished between the sixth and eighth centuries BC produced tartan-like textiles. Some were discovered in the Hallstatt saltines near Salzburg in a 2004 dig.

What makes ours special is how ownership of tartan has bounced between high society and subculture. Queen Victoria and Prince Albert both wore tartan during their trips to Scotland and later decorated Balmoral Castle with tartan floor coverings and accessories. Following these royal examples, the world went wild for our version of plaid, and tartanware soon became a fixture of homes around the UK. Later, in the 1970s, it was adopted as a symbol of anarchy by punks in ways that echoed the rebellious stance of Highlanders. Bondage kilts teamed with overt hostility to societal norms were the hallmarks of early Vivienne Westwood. Now no one bats an eye at a Conservative prime minister clad in one of her tartan trouser suits.

Recent adaptations of tartan include Samantha McCoach's Le Kilt, a brand founded in 2012. Her punk-laced riffs on the classic kilt have won favour with clients including Kate Middleton, proving further the cyclical nature of fashion. Meanwhile, families across the country continue to wear more traditionally styled kilts and tartan trousers in their clan colours at weddings and Highland games.

TWEED

Tweed was created by islanders on the Outer Hebrides to protect them from harsh winters. Using their own wool, crofters hand-wove clò mór, or "the big cloth". By the end of the eighteenth century, tweed had been identified as a key source of income and was exported to the mainland.

At the same time, tweed was also being produced in the Scottish Borders thanks to the myriad rivers that provided a source of energy for mills and ease of movement for materials. As the name suggests, one of the main transport arteries was the River Tweed, the 97-mile stretch of water connecting Scotland and northern England.

Tweed has since been adopted as a water-resistant material with which to make uniforms for estate workers who needed hardwearing outerwear to protect them from nettles, thorny bushes and mud. Estates would differentiate their tweeds from their neighbours' by commissioning local weavers to come up with patterns that drew from key elements of nature on their land.

Harris Tweed has gone global since the turn of the century: the brand has created fabrics for Chanel, Converse and Nike, and there are now all kinds of accessories made from the cloth – diversification being a cornerstone of survival and success.

If the hills on an estate shimmered with heather there might
be fine purple or russet thread running through its tweed.

FAIR ISLE KNIT

The classic Fair Isle jumper bears a few distinctive traits. It is hand-knitted with the traditional "in the round" method using double-pointed needles known locally as "wires", along with a special padded knitting belt, then dried over a wooden frame. A limited palette of about five colours is used.

Fair Isle knitwear is also an artefact of Shetland's socio-economic history. As far fewer men returned from the Second World War than went out to fight, Shetland women had to shift their knitting skills from hobby to income generator and rely on jumpers to keep their families afloat financially. In this way, the war acted as a force for good in that islanders began selling directly to servicemen stationed on the islands, a practice that would continue well into the 1940s. This meant they could achieve higher prices for their knitting, as they were cutting out the middle merchants, thereby controlling their own businesses.

On the runway, Ralph Lauren, Karl Lagerfeld and Burberry have all rehashed the classic Fair Isle design. Back on the island, the Fair Isle legacy is continued by a clutch of islanders who have formed a cooperative to safeguard the future of the island's knitting. Their coorie jumpers, which take at least three weeks to create, can command waiting lists of up to two years.

For the novice knitter, the Fair Isle style is a skill that can be mastered, but not without considerable determination. Knitting is a craft deeply embedded in Scottish culture, one that requires patience and commitment. Go fast and you risk a day's stitches. Take your time and the coorie yield awaits. **c**

Coorie Style 13

For a country with such a strong textile history, Scottish style is a little more muddled. Scots don't subscribe to a single look – it's more difficult to link to specific items than say, Danish women and their top-knotted hair, or Italian men and their penchant for fancy footwear.

However, generally speaking, those in the west tend to be a little more adventurous. To spot art-school boys with bowl cuts and blue lipstick head to Nice N Sleazy, a cult bar on Glasgow's Sauchiehall Street. Or for the city's famously glamorous ladies try the Corinthian. I want them to teach me how they apply their makeup so perfectly.

In contrast, you'd be lucky to see a pair of high heels in an Edinburgh pub on a Friday night. In their place are leather boots, coorie jumpers and a minimalist aesthetic.

When it comes to fashion designers, Scotland is bursting at the seams. The likes of Holly Fulton, Jonathan Saunders and Christopher Kane have sent their wares down the world's most illustrious catwalks while also promoting Scotland in subtle ways. Spin-off products include Kane's collaboration with Lancôme – a limited edition lipgloss named Burns Night.

There are plenty of other designers following in their footsteps, full of the same flair and ambition. Here are just five.

Now playing

Franz Ferdinand – 'Eleanor Put Your Boots On'

KESTIN HARE

Kestin Hare comes from creative lineage. His father, an architect, and his mother, an interior designer, encouraged their young son's talent for drawing, but it was only in late adulthood Hare realised his full artistic potential. Now he runs an eponymous menswear brand from premises at Leith's Custom House, a waterside creative hub at Edinburgh's Shore district.

Hare's output is directly informed by the country in which he has worked all his life. All trousers are water resistant, and many designs are made using Harris Tweed given a contemporary update with fresh wide-leg styling. A recent partnership with the footwear brand Superga gave life to half-nettle, half-cotton sneakers that are completely waterproof.

Hare's two-storey shop at the Shore supports collaboration at every turn. Alongside his garments are wall prints from the Glasgow design house Risotto and minimalist watches by Instrmnt.

"It's important we try to complement [our work] with other products," he explains. "There is an opportunity to show off great design and brands who are committed to showing Scotland in a different light."

About 70 per cent of the brand's garments are made within the UK. Seams on Kestin Hare outerware are sewn in Cumbernauld, North Lanarkshire, while his knitwear comes from Annan, Dumfries & Galloway. The logistics of running a business with such a broad church of output means it is not always realistic to manufacture all his garments in Scotland, but that is something Hare hopes will soon change.

"For the past twenty years it's not been seen as cool to be a seamstress," he says. "But we are having a rebirth in provenance and making. People are producing things with their hands again."

HILARY GRANT

Hilary Grant could write a guidebook on how to recycle spent ideas. So she did – *Knitting from the North* reveals this Orkney-based designer's creative secrets in the form of patterns for her past-season hats, mittens and scarves.

Sharing her designs with the public doesn't mean that demand has waned for her more recent collections, however. Retailers in Japan, China and the US are clamouring to stock her pieces, which can emerge from inspiration found in places as disparate as shed doors or repetitions in nature.

Born in Ayrshire, Grant moved to the Orcadian island of Mainland with her partner to begin a design partnership in 2011. Their studio produces blankets, scarves, gloves and pom-pom topped hats, with wave-inspired shapes giving insight into the couple's setting.

"One of the things I like about living on Orkney is the sense of freedom you don't always get stuck in Glasgow or Edinburgh," Grant says. "You put yourself into isolation like a monk, but I find it really good for the creative process."

Orkney's central position within the tripod of Scotland, Iceland and Scandinavia has helped ground the aesthetic of Grant's work. There is a common thread of northern-ness uniting her collections, evidenced in the geographical names given to garments and colours borrowed from surf spray. Southern Scotland is accounted for too. Grant uses a family-run manufacturer in the Borders to produce all the studio's accessories, resulting in collections that share a lexicon in their weft.

"There seems to be a certain language to my work through the visual effects of blending colours against pattern," she says.

CECILIA STAMP

Not everyone could find beauty in a crumbling ecclesiastical college on the Firth of Clyde. But Cecilia Stamp isn't everyone. This Glasgow-based jeweller studied silver-smithing at Edinburgh College of Art before completing a Master's in printed textile design at Heriot Watt in Galashiels, and after a spell spent working as a designer for other brands decided to launch her own business. A bold move by a maker with single digit years in the industry.

"I decided to get back into jewellery making after realising how much I missed the process of experimenting with materials and making with my hands," she says. "My work originates from a love of the man-made, including machinery, packaging, and modernist architecture, such as St Peter's Seminary, in Cardross."

The daughter of the renowned architecture writer Gavin Stamp, Cecilia has long channelled her father's love of buildings into her own work. She recently created a range of rings inspired by Alexander "Greek" Thomson, the Glasgow architect working in the mid nineteenth century, a man whose works her father established a society dedicated to.

Now, the Thomson-inspired pieces sit alongside earrings and necklaces made from enamel and precious metals. The designer isn't afraid to take on subject matters some consider off limits either, and it is this boldness of approach that sees her work subvert perceptions of jewellery as mere adornment.

"One of my first collections explored the graphic design of feminine sanitary packaging," she says. "It sparked a love for exploring imagery of unappealing source material and translating it into something desirable."

TRAKKE

The first time Alec Farmer drove through the Highlands he was hooked. Originally from Derbyshire, he relocated to Scotland to study graphic design at Glasgow School of Art, but admits he had "no idea we had such epic mountains in the UK. I was inspired to share that landscape".

A keen cyclist, Farmer designed a rudimentary messenger bag to withstand wind and rain that he could strap on his back while out on his bike. It worked so well that he made a couple of hundred, sold them on a tiny stall at the Barras, and got good feedback. *What next?* he wondered.

The answer was Trakke, an outdoor lifestyle brand. Dispel any notions of bland hiking gear: these are accessories created to retain their good looks and quality no many how many times you lug them up a mountain.

"We've swapped my living room for a huge workshop in Glasgow full of industrial machinery that enables us to make the best quality bags we can," Farmer says. "We now ship our range of backpacks and messenger bags across the world – from Antarctica to Asia and everywhere in between."

Trakke's waxed canvas bags are made from fabric manufactured in Dundee, the same kind of cloth invented by Scottish fishermen to help them stay dry while working out at sea. Stainless steel buckles are practically unbreakable and even the fibre of the products is made with super strong webbing.

His business's surroundings may have changed, but Farmer's ethos remains the same as the Barras market stall days. "When a group of people move in the same direction, they make a track," he says. "That's the idea behind our brand."

MATI VENTRILLON

In a previous life Mati Ventrillon worked as an architect in her home country of Venezuela. Now she revives historic Shetland knitting techniques from Fair Isle, the most remote inhabited island in the UK.

With a population of just fifty-one residents, Fair Isle and its crofts are a far cry from the tropical climes of South America.

Still, Ventrillon was attracted to its remote beauty, and began working with social historians to discover more about the island's textile heritage.

"Knitting has happened here continuously for more than two hundred years and I became more and more curious as I tried to understand the background of the island," she says. "I fell in love with it and I decided that this was what I was going to do."

For a year she attended a weekly workshop in London and spent seven days a month in England learning how to run her new business, followed by three weeks back on Fair Isle raising her two children.

The sacrifice paid off. When she launched her own company, the designer noted there were no Fair Isle jumpers for consumers to buy online, so her initial plan was to rectify that.

Ventrillon's patterns draw from original 1850s designs with Shetland wool spun on 1960s knitting machines to make jerseys, known as ganzies. Now that her own firm is established, Ventrillon has turned her thoughts back to the community.

"The idea is to continue passing on these skills," she says. "We want to show there is an alternative to leaving university and college and going straight to a fashion house." ℮

The Makers of Coorie   14

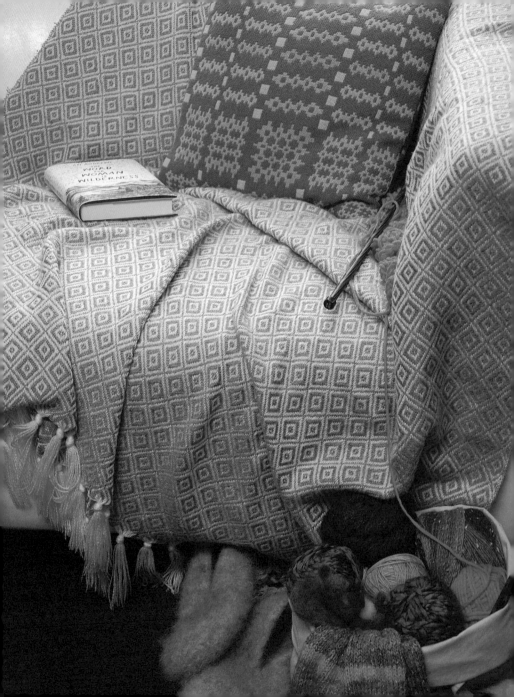

A coorie home is one that both looks and feels good. A squishy couch and a favourite mug filled with a steaming cup of tea can brighten the edges of even the most miserable day. There must be a psychological reason behind why we get attached to certain items in our homes, whether it's dad's armchair with its alarmingly permanent bum groove, or a wooden spoon with just the right shaped handle. Answers on a postcard, please.

Coorie interiors are ones that lift the spirits. Sterile or overly cluttered spaces aren't very coorie because they don't make us want to spend time there with the people we love. Designers such as Alistair MacAuley and Paul Simmons, the brains behind Timorous Beasties, are bringing panache to homes around the world with their maximalist wallpapers and fabrics. Their designs feature thistles – that enduring mascot – but also high-rise flats and urban decay. How they interpret what's around them shows coorie homes can be filled with the unexpected and still be our own. The following up-and-coming designers are also unafraid to defy convention.

"Coorie is like a wee cuddle, either with a person or in a blanket."

CATHERINE JOHNSTON

Catherine Johnston is a woman of the woods. Not only does this multi-discipline designer make tableware out of timber, she also wields the material to teach others about the natural world.

Johnston's firm, Object Company, came out of a simple desire to work with her hands. In order to do so she sourced an arboriculturist close to Mount Florida Gallery and Studios, in Glasgow, which she founded in 2014. Wood from felled trees in the city's parks and gardens is gathered and sold to makers such as Johnston, a pleasing continuum of the usefulness of nature. Then she considered her aesthetic – minimalism was key, but she also required her pieces to have tactility.

"The trees have rarely been well-kept and offer the most beautiful, if challenging irregularities," Johnston explains. "The wood often reflects the landscape, as the trees are allowed to grow organically, to become gnarly and irregularly shaped due to the harsh and often extreme weather."

Once smaller planks of wood are cut from the logs, each piece is carefully assessed to form the starting point of a project. Once Johnston has decided on the piece she will slowly air dry the wood, cut it out, shape it and finish it, all by hand.

Ebonised oak, wych elm and holly turn into scoop-sets, chopping boards, butter spreaders and serving spoons. "Each piece is designed with a purpose in mind," she says of her work. "I only make objects that will contribute positively to the basics of everyday life."

Teaching others about this process is at the heart of Object Company's output. Johnston also hosts workshops in which participants gain skills in knife and axe work.

"Scotland has such varied terrain and landscapes.
With this comes plenty of variety in smellscapes, too."

LaB_6 CANDLES

Candles might be the epitome of hygge, but Scots can more than hold their own when it comes to making little objects of wax alchemy.

After working in clinical laboratories for decades, Murray Hamilton felt a career change in the air.

"LaB_6 started as a chance experiment and has grown into a passion," he says. "It took nearly a year for me to refine the making process and it was important for me that the main signature fragrances reflected my love and memories of my favourite places in Scotland."

He's not kidding. Stick a nose into any of his candles to visualise the Cairngorms after rainfall, or kelp drying on the rocks of a Hebridean beach.

In a world where the home fragrance market has become oversaturated, Hamilton wants to keep life simple. His starting point is to work out which scents encountered in everyday life work best in the home, then apply the necessary methods to take each smell from landscape to laboratory.

All LaB_6 candles begin life as fragrance oil blends and mineral wax flakes. After combining ingredients and heating them, the mixture is poured by hand into recycled glass science beakers, the kind you may recognise from your school days, and allowed to set.

"Wandering through Highland pine forests and on island beaches or simply stepping into my grandfather's garden with his soft fruits growing: these are the smells that I love and want in my home," the former scientist explains.

ARAMINTA CAMPBELL

Many of today's tweeds have been around for almost two hundred years, a throwback to a time where hand power was king. Araminta Campbell is ensuring the future of these textiles remains old school, while bringing them in line with modern tastes.

The Aberdeenshire-born weaver believes in a loom of one's own; and hers is more than a hundred years old. It is responsible for the delicate cashmere cushions, scarves and shawls she sells from her online store, and also for bespoke tweed she is commissioned to create by clients around Scotland.

Clans whose tweed has not been altered in centuries ask Campbell to draw inspiration from the landscape of their estates and reflect the colours she sees into a refreshed design. These new fabrics can then be turned into uniforms, homeware or upholstery fabrics upon the estate's request.

"I see myself as developing new ways of doing old things – using the best of the past to create beautiful pieces that will be loved in the present and the future," Campbell explains. "It's about valuing style over trend, and making products that will stand the test of time."

More recently, she has expanded her line to include ultra luxurious items, as part of her signature Minta range. Undyed alpaca fleeces sourced from around the UK are spun and woven at mills in the Borders.

Her hand-woven products balance and blend form with function; despite their down-soft texture they are built to last. "My pieces are made to be used and enjoyed," Campbell says. "I like to encourage taking time to appreciate and understand the process behind my work, which is something I think people are increasingly searching for."

NATALIE J. WOOD

You don't need to leave Scotland to produce ceramics with global influence. That theory permeates the work of Natalie J. Wood from Kirkcaldy, in Fife, who studied three-dimensional design at Gray's School of Art, Aberdeen.

"Most people see my work and think it's a mix of Japanese and Scandinavian," Wood says. "But I have never been to Japan and only travelled to Denmark last year."

Without the opportunity to leave Scotland, Wood imagined how her travels might inform her ceramics. Romanticising about cultures she had not experienced led to her first body of work, Detsu, a tableware set comprising brightly coloured vessels, jugs and plates.

Working with clay allows the designer to reference the past – slip-casting techniques have remained unchanged in centuries – while also drinking up the world around her. Life experiences give Wood further room to expand and explore: her friends describe her as pragmatic, and it's this trait that's absorbed most apparently into her work.

Adding to "throwaway culture", as Wood calls it, is a practice she tries to avoid, because of the inflexible nature of finished clay.

"It's difficult to recycle ceramics after they are fired: they become a permanent fixture lasting many lifetimes," she explains. "I try to respect that by taking the time to think of the William Morris quote – 'Have nothing in your house that you do not know to be useful, or believe to be beautiful.'"

Wood has cultivated an aesthetic that borrows from Japanese minimalism but remains bound up in Scottish identity.

IONA CRAWFORD

Lying on the forest floor with her eyes trained on a canopy of trees above, a young Iona Crawford had no idea she was sowing the seeds for her adult career as a luxury homeware designer.

Two decades later and her love for the world around her hasn't waned, but she also bears a new talent: the ability to trust her instinct in business.

"During my university studies at Edinburgh College of Art my parents encouraged me to spend time on our farm drawing livestock and birds, which was challenging," she says. "In the end, I decided to take all the figurative life drawing out of my final submission portfolio and put in my farm life drawings. They were part of my roots."

It's staying true to her roots that has enabled Crawford's boldly printed wallpapers and lush fabrics to delight clients in the US and at home.

In her latest collection, the kaleidoscopic Wilderness wallpaper references treescapes seen from the ground of the Barr Wood, in Stirling, close to where she grew up.

She recently collaborated with the Michelin-starred chef Andrew Fairlie to come up with Our Secret Garden, a line of homeware inspired by the fruit and vegetables growing at a preserved Victorian kitchen garden in Perthshire. Linen, screen-printed velvet and the finest suede make up the fabric arm of Crawford's brand, while wall coverings in painterly patterns envelop a room, dressing the space as fluidly as if it were a body.

"I love how you can take something two-dimensional and translate it into a three-dimensional piece," the designer says. "It allows me to look at print in a different way, almost adding a fourth dimension." ℮

Coorie Hideouts 15

Waking up to the sight of dawn breaking over one of Scotland's Munros is the kind of medicine that should be available on the NHS.

It's the combination of country air and no phone reception that does it for me. If I want to stay inside my lochside cabin cooried in on a dreich day with a trashy magazine there's no stopping me. The same goes for getting up early, pulling back the curtains and feeling the morning rays on my face. Then it might be the perfect opportunity for hill running – either observing or taking part – especially in places such as Sligachan on the Isle of Skye. It hosts the Glamaig summer hill race, which sees participants from all over the world make the gruelling ascent up 2,500 feet for four miles of torture – and the rhapsodic feeling of pounding over the finish line. Hobble back to your cottage after a post-race pint in the Sligachan Hotel for a well-deserved bowl of mac and cheese and a midnight star spotting session.

Being a tourist in our own country opens up parts of Scotland we never knew existed. New places to stay the night spring up every month; some remain a guarded secret and others are booked up months in advance. These are some of my favourites.

Now playing

Jesus and Mary Chain – 'The Hardest Walk'

AIRSHIP 002

Drimnin, the Highlands

When you have an idea that's completely out of this world, seeing it through to the end requires determination. Happily, the architect Roderick James is a person who has this trait etched into his DNA. In 2010 he dreamed up a way of bringing the bothy into the twenty-first century when he pitched to win a contract to design wild cabins. Keen to conceive a building that would not degrade, James translated the bothy's traditional wooden walls and floor into an intergalactic aluminium spaceship. The space had to be warm and functional, but the rest, he felt, was open to interpretation.

The pitch wasn't successful, but James's plans were far from over. AirShip 002, comprising more than three thousand pieces, was constructed on top of a mountain edge in the northwest Highlands. This unique cabin will not rot, rust, or be adversely affected by the weather.

AirShip 002 is accessed from a small path shrouded by shrubs that clear to reveal a stainless steel pod with a glazed nose and rear. The mainland is so close to the Isle of Mull you can see the silhouette of trees across the water from the terrace.

Within, the vibe is modern and calm. A double bed is set flush to one wall shielded from the living area with a curtain, creating a Russian doll effect of a coorie zone within a coorie zone. On one side are portholes through which you can stargaze as you fall asleep.

The AirShip is plumbed, wired and lit, the kitchen has a microwave oven and the bathroom a good-sized shower. Yet the feeling of wilderness doesn't suffer from these modern privileges. You only need to listen to the owls or watch a storm whip up the Sound of Mull to remind you that while sleek design is keeping you safe, Scotland at its most wild is on the other side of the glass.

NATURAL RETREATS
AT JOHN O' GROATS

John o' Groats, Caithness

Perched on the most northeasterly tip of Scotland, a settlement of twenty-three lodges rises out of the stark landscape. These self-catered pods neighbour Natural Retreats John o' Groats, a whitewashed Scots baronial building originally constructed in 1875 and meticulously upgraded in 2013 to become a £6.5 million hotel.

Feature walls and accessories in the self-catered flats, lodges and hotel rooms have been upholstered in Harris Tweed and a chandelier in the main foyer started life as lobster creels once submerged off the Caithness coast. If that doesn't give you enough of a clue about location, rope lights were knotted by a local fisherman on site specifically for the building.

GLM Architects added a rainbow extension to the main building and clad lodges in Scottish-grown larch manufactured in Inverness. Both are designed to withstand wind headed straight from the Arctic circle, with floor-to-ceiling windows giving big-sky views of the Pentland Firth and out to Orkney.

Natural Retreats had its work cut out imbuing character into the site but by sprinkling the right number of personal touches, interior designers created a hip space that also feels homely. Artwork and photography displayed in public areas illustrate the building's story, while magnified domes set at child height encourage exploration.

There's an on-site shop bearing some local fare, but the trick is to stock up on supplies in Wick (sixteen miles) or Thurso (nineteen miles) before you arrive. Then you can spend your days walking, reading, or visiting the Puffin Croft petting farm in the village, where you can hang out with Chickpea and Cauliflower the goats.

It's worth navigating the stony beach to pick up the path beginning at the Duncansby Head lighthouse – follow the clifftop to see the Stacks of Duncansby and their soaring rock formations. In the evening, fire up the log-burning stove and watch the landscape outside as night darkens the corners of the sky.

COORIE TIP: Lodges 22 and 23 have the best views of the Pentland Firth.

GUARDSWELL FARM

Kinnaird, Perthshire

A family business can mean one of two careers. The burden of inheriting a job not suited to your skill set, or the opportunity to feed off multi-generational experience and work with the people you love. In the case of Guardswell Farm, the Lamotte family find themselves happily in the latter situation.

Mum, Dad, aunties, and daughter Anna take on the various roles needed to run this high-end rural idyll, which features a bothy, cabin, converted steading and farmhouse. Even Mole, the springer spaniel, forms an integral part of the crew, approaching guests and wagging her tail so violently it threatens to propel her into the air.

"Coorie-in is what my mum would always say when she was tucking me into bed. I say that in the past tense, but she still insists on it!"

The Lamottes' tie to the area spans back many generations, but in 2014 they met architects Rosemary and Ben Scrimgeour of the Building Workshop and came up with a plan for the future. The family commissioned the couple to draw up a community of buildings that could host relaxed weddings, soothe jaded urbanites looking for a rest, and provide parents an off-grid space in which they could regroup with their children.

Working closely together, the Lamottes and the Scrimgeours transformed Guardswell's former agricultural buildings into glossy magazine-worthy structures, where sheepskins from the farm serve as functional decoration alongside brass candlesticks, simple timber furniture, and books on art, lifestyle and nature. Guests can help themselves to vegetables grown in the Kailyard, or pick flowers from the grounds.

Perhaps the star of Guardswell Farm is the Infield, a black larch clad cabin sleeping four that the Scrimgeours designed to jut out from the hill and look out over Dundee and Fife. The building's glazed gable end leads out to a balcony strung with agricultural wire as a nod to the farm's former life. What elevates this hut above the standard timber job is one key ingredient that's near impossible to buy: good taste. Who would have thought that a pair of yellow hot-water bottles hanging on the wall could make such a chic design statement? The Lamottes, and thank goodness they did.

MONACHYLE MHOR

Balquhidder, Perthshire

In the restaurant trade where colourful characters are two a penny, the word "maverick" crops up all too often. But in the case of Tom Lewis it is justified, thanks to the chef's singular outlook on Scottish food and hospitality.

When Lewis and his wife Lisa launched Monachyle Mhor, a boutique farmhouse with luxurious rooms, they were joined by Lewis's brother, Dick, and his wife, Mhairi Taylor, the brains behind Glasgow's Delizique café.

Together the team wanted to create the ultimate pit stop between southern and northern Scotland, a place of foodie pilgrimage where

Now playing

Tony McManus – 'The Lament for the Viscount of Dundee'

hungry travellers could pause for breath, eat local goodies and bed down for the night.

What they created goes beyond that initial vision. Today, a range of sleeping spaces is on offer; the cooriest found in the millennial-pink period farmhouse where the Lewises grew up.

Rooms feature reclaimed wooden ladders that double as hanging space for clothes, clapboard headboards and a mixture of old (vintage nightstands) and new (Hans Wegner chairs) furniture.

If Monachyle Mhor farmhouse functions as the site's chic older sister, the cabin is the younger sibling after a sugar overdose. This brilliantly bonkers residence started life as a waiting room at Port Appin ferry terminal, but once the Lewises heard it was heading for the tip they stepped in to save it.

With the help of two architecture students it was turned into a super-cool hut with plywood walls, picture frame windows and Muuto "Hang it All" coat hooks. Next door is a bothy with a corrugated tin roof which was given a refresh with minimalist styling. They are rented as a pair sleeping four.

A childlike playfulness permeates through both buildings, the same kind that Tom Lewis pours into his own work. You can't help but take life less seriously during a stay here.

THE PINEAPPLE

Dunmore, Stirlingshire

You might find a toadstool in a Scottish forest, or horse chestnuts, or brambles. But a pineapple? Only in Dunmore, near Falkirk in Stirlingshire.

This whimsical folly flanked by stone cottages is one of nineteen properties on long lease to the Landmark Trust, the charity that restored it from a wreck to a retreat.

The Pineapple's architect is unknown, but what is certain is who commissioned it. In 1761 the Fourth Earl of Dunmore had been married for two years; some speculate the folly was built for him as a belated wedding gift, or to commemorate the fertile nature of the Dunmore Estate's vegetable garden.

Now its curling stone leaves delight guests who stay here every year and walkers who can view its exterior from the far side of the buildings.

Arrival to the Pineapple up a narrow winding road in the dark is the stuff of creepy movies. All spookiness melts away once inside, however: the octagonal fruit has been turned into a sweet summerhouse with pared-back living space in each cottage including that coorie essential – a large wood-burning stove.

Distinctive touches can be spotted throughout the Pineapple. There's a vintage book cabinet stuffed with titles on subjects the building is known for, such as the history of the folly or birds that make their home in the neighbouring forest.

But it's the Pineapple's uniqueness that is its real draw. It is a purely ornamental structure, gleeful in its exuberance. Scotland's architectural pedigree is enriched by it. **c**

COORIE TIP: Take a pair of cosy baffies to wear for the brief outside walk between the two living spaces, which are connected by an external stone staircase.

Thrifty Coorie   16

If the best things in life are free,

the second-best things cost

only a handful of pennies

The first time I was interviewed on TV about coorie, a question was thrown my way that made me query the concept's universal appeal. The presenter asked me whether coorie could be construed as a purely middle-class pursuit, in other words, a way of living that excluded anyone who did not have a decent chunk of disposable time and money.

Those were the early days of coorie entering the mainstream, so it was hardly surprising that people queried what it was really about. Speaking to people in the creative industries had shown me that choosing coorie as part of your life wasn't about having lots of cash, but maybe that wasn't as obvious to others.

With that in mind, I began to think about the cooriest activities that cost little or no money. Because coorie believes in looking out for ways to make the most of what's around us, creating coorie on the cheap is easy. An added bonus of many of these coorie activities is that they force us to slow down and ask deeper questions about where we are going and where we have been. They also encourage collaboration, whether that's spending time with our nieces and nephews baking cakes, taking our dogs for a walk, combing the beach for shells, or chatting to older generations about the history of our country.

There are countless ways to embody coorie into your days at work, days off, nights in the city and nights out in the wild. The following ideas to create coorie should point you in the right direction, and the how-to guides will give you ideas for a coorie project of your own.

FERN AND FLOWER PRESSING

Inspecting flora for rare ferns or Scots lovage flower heads sprinkled like a constellation in the grass is guaranteed to clear the mind. It's also a chance to learn more about the natural world. Take your forest finds home and press between the pages of a book (one with thin, crepe-y paper works best for blotting). Wait a month and you're ready to put your pressing into a hanging glass case or tape it to birthday cards. You can also track the seasons in a scrapbook of pressed flowers. Start in January and see what you discover throughout the year.

HOST A POT LUCK DINNER

Nominate a friend with the cooriest home – and promise to help them with setting up and clearing away – then arrange a night where everyone is free for dinner. The only rule is that all diners must bring a dish. You can theme the evening by season or ingredient, or by a particular memory. Try a root vegetable themed banquet in autumn or dishes originating from each person's home county (or country). The beauty of a pot luck dinner is that, save for dinner plates and cutlery, there's minimal washing up and mess for the host to deal with after guests have cleared off with their receptacles. The cooriest pot luck dinner should see kids tasting new flavours, grandparents regaling the table with stories and the family's best chef showing off about their latest piece of kit.

GO SWIMMING

There's an otherworldly sense evoked when submerging your body into water. Over the years I've swum in private members' clubs, my local leisure pool and lochs, depending on how much money I had at any given point. Swimming is a mental cleanser and feels somehow timeless. You can lose whole chunks of an afternoon under the water's surface.

While I love the steamy windows of Glasgow's Arlington Baths and the charm of Leith's Victorian swim centre on Junction Place, my favourite has to be the open sea. To me, outdoor swimming as exercise feels different to any other kind of physical exertion. It connects you with nature and you feel pure, reborn even. Scotland's wild swimming spots are also the perfect antidote to screen time. At a fitness class or jogging I struggle not to check my phone. When swimming, it stays safely on dry land.

My cousin and I once spent a week in the Western Isles and swam in the Atlantic, off the coast of North Uist. It was mid January, and although we were blessed with temperatures nudging ten degrees we were knocked to the shore and half drowned in waist-high water because of the sea's raw energy. Our swim, and the blissful feeling of thawing out in the car and ravenously munching biscuits afterwards, were the highlights of our trip. Scots even have a phrase for a post-swim snack – a "shivery piece" or "shivery bite", otherwise known as a sandwich spread with jam or margarine.

I stumbled upon a memory posted online by Margaret Cooper, a former resident of Edinburgh, about her own shivery bite consumed after "almost drowning" at Warrender Park Baths in the 1940s. "I managed to get out, greetin'," she said. "I went to my wee cubicle, ate my shivery bite and ten minutes later I was back in for more."

CHECK OUT 'DOORS OPEN DAY'

It's easy to make the same journey every day
and pledge to find out what's behind an unusual
door or façade then forget to do it. Doors Open
Day seeks to provide that knowledge by feeding
the minds of the curious. Every weekend in
September, more than a thousand buildings
around Scotland that are usually off limits to the
public throw open their doors. Structures range
from a private telephone museum housed within
a former bakehouse in Ayrshire, to an Art Deco
fire station in Aberdeen where children (and
adults) can meet the engine fleet.

Scotland's Gardens, the charity, also opens
the gates to the country's most beautiful private
gardens – from back yards to grand country
houses – at select times throughout the year.

"I went to my wee cubicle, ate my shivery bite and
ten minutes later I was back in for more."

LEARN TO KNIT

Raid charity shops for yarn, needles and vintage patterns – all the bits you need to start can be picked up for a couple of pounds. Then, enlist the help of a friendly expert – online or in person – to give you a steer before beginning a simple design. The aim is a Mrs Weasley-style scarf you can relax while knitting, rather than a haute couture woollen gown glinting with tears of frustration.

CARE FOR A HOUSE PLANT

Scotland, along with the rest of the UK, is in the grips of a house plant epidemic. Swiss cheese plants are threatening to take over bathrooms, while fragile pileas spill over mantles and windowsills in every lust-worthy flat on Instagram. Caring for our green chums is a bit like looking after a pet. We need to live with them a while and discover their idiosyncrasies before they can thrive.

The short days in winter and cold temperatures can make it hard for house plants to flourish in Scotland, but getting to know each variety and how they exist best in your home is vital to working out why wilting or yellowing happens.

HOW TO MAKE A COORIE GARDEN GROTTO
£50

Everyone needs a space in which they can hide from the world. But it's not always easy to have one in your house. The ideal scenario is to have a room away from the main thoroughfare of a home – and that's where a garden room comes in handy.

My idea for a coorie garden grotto came from a visit to the Secret Herb Garden, a seven-acre site outside of Edinburgh at the foot of the Pentland Hills.

While wandering about I clocked an incredible grotto made by draping lopped-off branches over a structure. It got me thinking how a more permanent arrangement could be managed.

The below guide assumes you have a shed or a simple summerhouse to begin with, but you can also start without one and plant bamboo in a semicircle, then train it to grow upwards – and feel the pleasure of seeing it grow. Inside you can get to work making the space as coorie as you like with soft lighting, cushions, a bench and a table, while a fire pit can be created outside. It's probably not the best idea to keep your decorations out overnight, though. No one likes a soggy bottom.

What you will need
- Vigorous climbers. Anything from sweet peas and honeysuckle, to bamboo, Virginia Creeper or ivy. The light and wind the space receives will determine what can be grown.
- 30m of 2mm PVC coated garden wire
- 75mm screw in vine eyes

Here's how to do it

1 Cut a series of taut horizontal and vertical wires dependent on the height and length of your shed walls. Place them 50mm off the wall, 450mm apart with the first wire 300mm above the soil level. Fix the wires to the shed with the vine eyes.

2 Choose your climbers. They will come in a pot already growing up bamboo canes.

3 To train them onto the support framework, plant the climber and its supporting bamboo canes 30 to 45mm away from the face of the shed so that the plant will catch the rain and has room for the roots to develop.

4 Remove the ties that hold the climber to its bamboo supports and lean three bamboo supports towards the shed, tucking them behind the newly fixed horizontal and vertical wire framework in a fan shape. Carefully tie the plant stems and supporting canes to your new wire framework and prune any twiggy growth. Tie in new growth regularly until the plant is established.

5 For speedy results, try sweet peas, nasturtiums, or runner beans to provide a harvest. But as these are annual plants, they will die at summer's end.

6 Perennial plants grow more established each year, but are easy to cut back with garden shears or secateurs when they get too big and bushy.

HOW TO MAKE A FACE SCRUB
WITH PORRIDGE OATS
5p

Years ago, a colleague told me a story about
her beauty journalist friend who eschewed
expensive facial scrubs for a homemade version
that contained oats. Mind blown. One of the
most basic ingredients, the simple porridge oat
is now being adopted by experts to practise
self-care. This scrub mix is dead simple, and
you're likely to already have both ingredients in
your cupboard. Your skin will thank you and your
wallet will too.

You will need
- 2 tbsp ground rolled oats
- 1 tbsp of honey

To make
1   In a small bowl, mix the oatmeal and
    honey. Larger oats can be ground down
    using a coffee grinder or blender.

2   Add 1 tbsp warm water and mix so it
    becomes a paste.

3   Apply scrub to entire face with
    fingertips and massage for one minute,
    then let it sit for five minutes.

4   Rinse off with a flannel and warm water.

HOW TO MAKE A COORIE CAKE
£3

Baking has always been a bit of a mystery to me. Cooking is great because you can freestyle and it usually makes the dish better, but cakes are scientific and demand much more time and concentration. That was my theory until I tried this recipe, written for *The Art of Coorie* by Flora Shedden. Flora was one of the breakout stars of *The Great British Bake Off*, and has since gone on to open the uber-coorie Aran Bakery in her hometown of Dunkeld, in Perthshire. Here she puts together some store cupboard essentials and comes up with one of the cooriest – and most fail-safe – cakes I've ever baked.

Ingredients for the Earl Grey fruit
- 300ml water
- 150g sultanas or raisins
- 2 Earl Grey tea bags

For the cake
- 225g unsalted butter, well softened
- 225g light brown sugar
- 225g self-raising flour
- 4 large eggs
- 2 tbsp honey
- 1 tsp mixed spice
- Zest of 1 lemon
- 75g flaked almonds

For the icing
- 200g icing sugar
- 100g butter
- 2 tbsp honey
- Flaked almonds

Method

1 Preheat the oven to 180°C. Grease and line a loose-bottomed 20cm cake tin.

2 Begin with the Earl Grey fruit. In a saucepan add the water, fruit and tea bags. Bring to the boil and allow to simmer until the water is reduced by half and the fruit plump and soft. Set aside to cool completely.

3 In the bowl of a free-standing mixer beat the butter, sugar, flour, eggs, honey and mixed spice together until light and fluffy. I find a whisk attachment works best.

4 Fold through the lemon and almonds. Drain the cooled fruit and remove the tea bags. Fold through the cake mixture, then spoon into the prepared tin. Bake for fifty minutes or until golden and a skewer inserted into the middle comes out clean. Set aside to cool.

5 To finish, toast a few handfuls of flaked almonds in a pan over a low to medium heat. Stir regularly to avoid burning. Once golden and nutty-smelling, remove.

6 For the icing, place the butter, icing sugar and honey into the bowl of a free-standing mixer and whip on a high speed until white and very light in consistency. Spread over the cooled cake, smoothing the edges then scatter with the toasted nuts.

7 Serve with a steaming cup of Earl Grey for a decadent afternoon tea.

HOW TO MAKE YOUR OWN GIN
£15

Scotland now accounts for 40 per cent of the UK's gin export production – not bad for a liquor that, until the late noughties, was synonymous with London. One of the reasons behind this Caledonian gin boom is the ease with which it is made. Unlike its malty cousin, gin needs only to distil with its botanicals for about six weeks before it's ready to drink. This makes it very appealing to independent gin producers.

It is even quicker and easier to make gin at home. It relies on the same components as shop-bought gin, but the recipe comes together in a different way. Instead of distilling botanicals to extract their flavours, bootleg gin sees them steep in liquid. This is known as compound gin.

Possibly the best thing about DIY gin is that you get to add whatever you fancy to taste. Consider pine needles for more citrus, chilli for a kick, lavender for floral notes or rosemary for earthiness. The latter three ingredients can be grown in a simple windowbox, while the former is foraged from the woods. When your gin is distilled, you can invite your friends over for a coorie cocktail masterclass and bask in your newfound popularity.

Ingredients
- 75cl vodka
- 2 tbsp juniper berries (minimum)
- 1 tsp coriander seeds
- Pinch of dried angelica root
- 2 cardamom pods
- 2 peppercorns, pink or black
- A small piece of citrus peel: grapefruit, lemon, orange or lime (no pith)

Method
1 Add the base flavours to a clean glass bottle with a suitable stopper.

2 Add vodka.

3 Leave to steep in a cool place for at least 24 hours.

4 Add peel and any other additional botanicals that take your fancy.

5 Leave for another 24 hours – shake the bottle gently once.

6 Taste the infusion. If it needs more time to steep, leave for another 12 hours but don't over-stew; it's a delicate drink you're after.

7 Remove the solids by straining the liquid through a piece of fine fabric.

8 Strain again after the gin has sat for another 48 hours.

9 Bottle, label and serve.

HOW TO EXTRACT ESSENCE FROM PINE NEEDLES
Free

Scottish pine needle oil, or essence, can be added to food and cocktails to give an alpine sweetness.

There are a couple of ways to incorporate pine needles into cooking. The easiest is to dry the needles completely, whizz in a blender and sprinkle as a powdered garnish on to puddings. Infusing them into dry cure rubs or alcohol is also straightforward. This method features Grand Fir and Douglas Fir needles harvested fresh from the forest floor.

Humans + fire + food

= happiness

1 Gather pine needles – the fresher and greener the better. Aim for about three bags of branches.

2 Strip needles from the branches and wash thoroughly with a mild soap in a bowl of hot water. Rinse needles well before blotting with paper towels.

3 Place clean needles in a mortar and bruise with a pestle. You may need to do this in batches for large quantities.

4 Add bruised needles to salt or sugar and leave to infuse for two weeks before using this as the base for curing meat and fish.

5 Or you can add the needles to a flavourless alcohol, such as vodka, and leave to infuse for at least a month.

HOW TO SMOKE YOUR OWN FOOD
£5

Smoking is up there with the world's most primitive cooking methods.

There's little need to buy a pricey home smoker when you can make a rudimentary one yourself. Smoking food is done via two methods – hot and cold. The former cooks moist food such as meat, fish and vegetables in the heat of the smoke, while the latter infuses cool smoke through cheese, garlic, salt, nuts and butter to add flavour. Here is a guide to make a small hot smoker – the cold version is a little more difficult as it involves running a length of bendy spiral ducting to siphon smoke from one chamber to another.

A DIY hot smoker lends itself well to coorie camping and other outdoor trips, when heavy, expensive gear isn't handy. A designated smoke supervisor happy to stay at camp can keep an eye on the food while everyone else heads off for a walk. Come dusk, a smoked feast awaits.

You will need
- A large, lidded empty metal tin; the kind that once contained Christmas sweets is perfect
- A metal grid; the kind that can be removed from disposable barbecues
- Wood shavings; beech, oak or applewood smoke well
- Tin foil

Method
1 Prepare your fish or poultry by covering it lightly with ordinary table salt and leaving it to cure. For two 130g breasts of chicken or two 200g fillets of salmon or trout (oily fish works best) allow thirty minutes. Once cured, rinse off the salt and pat dry.

2 Place a couple of handfuls of wood chips or shavings on the bottom of the biscuit tin and lay a loose layer of foil on top. This will stop the juice from the food dripping on to the woodchips.

3 Pierce a couple of holes in the tin lid with a screwdriver. Put a rack in the tin so it sits half way down. Put your chicken on to the rack (place the fish skin down).

4 Place the tin lid or one made of tinfoil over the tin, securing tightly, and place on some hot coals or a gas stove on a high setting. When you start to see some smoke, turn the gas down a little to a medium setting and leave it to do its magic.

5 The two fillets of salmon should take between ten and fifteen minutes to smoke. The chicken needs longer so allow about thirty minutes. With a probe, check it can hold a temperature of 75°C for thirty seconds. If smoking vegetables, skewer after five minutes to see if they are cooked. **c**

Festive Coorie   **17**

For hundreds of years Christmas was a very quiet affair in Scotland. During the Protestant reformation, Oliver Cromwell banned Christ's Mass under the premise of its Catholic roots, and while the ban was only implemented for fifteen years in England, further north, the Scottish Presbyterian church continued to discourage celebrations until the early eighteenth century.

These days, there's nothing to stop the festivities. While Christmas in Scotland isn't so different from anywhere else in the world, how we incorporate the landscape of our lives into celebrations makes it coorie. This gives us an excuse to get off the couch and head into the garden or the park to go gathering foliage to dress our homes. In a month where winter malaise can kick in, having a creative project that involves being outside during daylight hours is welcome.

In order to get a good cross-section of opinions, I asked three women working in Scotland to tell me how they do Christmas. Their answers surprised me in different ways: each has a beautifully stylish home, but at Christmas their approach to decorating focuses on stirring up memories rather than immaculate planning.

The fun is galvanising the family and using Christmas as a way to kick start new traditions. What could be coorier than handing over gifts festooned with beautiful branches of fir, giving homemade wreaths to neighbours, or decorating a Christmas tree with your siblings by the hearth?

HOW TO MAKE A COORIE CHRISTMAS WREATH

Laura Thomas of Laura Thomas Linens

Evergreen foliage on a Christmas wreath is symbolic of the continuity of life and nature, even in the depths of a Scottish winter. The preparation stage is hunting and gathering resources in order to create your wreath. To keep it as fresh as possible, your main greenery will need to be sourced one or two days before making. Scotland is full of wild foliage and you're never too far away to collect your greenery.

You'll need

- Foliage
- Secateurs
- Green florist's wire on a reel, 26 / 28 gauge
- Pine cones
- Cinnamon sticks
- Dried oranges
- Ribbon
- Circular florist foam oasis 16cm (or 12 / 14cm as desired)

How to prep

1 Dry the pine cones on newspaper near a heat source for at least five days to ensure they have no moisture in them. Once dry, cut 15cm of florist wire. Fit the wire around and within the outer edges of the bottom of the pine cone. Create a tail by twisting the two strands of wire together. This will be used to push the cones into the foam of the oasis.

2 Dry your oranges. Thinly slice two oranges to about 3cm in width, disregarding the two ends. Place on a baking tray and put in the oven for three hours at 100°C. Turn every half hour. Cut 15cm of florist wire. Poke through the orange and again twist the two strands together to create a wire tail.

3 Group two to three cinnamon sticks together. Cut 15cm of florist wire and wrap around the sticks, twisting the wire together to create a tail.

4 Gather your foliage from neighbouring woods or your garden. For one wreath you'll need at least half a bucket full of fir as well as half a bucket of holly. The red berries look gorgeous on your wreath and give a good splash of traditional Christmas colour, so if you can find a tree with lots of berries get in quickly before the birds eat them. It is best to pick the holly at the end of November as by mid December there is not much left.

How to make

1 Wet your oasis before making your wreath. Once created, make sure to re-wet your wreath every two to three days to make it last well into January.

2 Attach your florist wire to the oasis. Your wire will not need to be cut until the very end of creating your wreath so don't be tempted. To attach, pull a length of 10cm out from the reel. Holding this wire tail with one hand, wrap the wire around the oasis five times with the other hand. It's fine for the wire to cut into the oasis. Once done, tuck the tail into the foam so it is no longer visible.

3　In the palm of your hand, fan out a couple of pieces of fir and lay some holly on top. Place it at an angle towards the centre of the ring and lay it down on the oasis. Secure to the oasis by wrapping the wire around the foliage two or three times. Do not stab the foliage onto the oasis, just lay it on top and wrap the wire around it.

4　Repeat step 3; but this time, lay the foliage at the opposite angle pointing outwards from the centre.

5　Repeat this process of one bundle facing inwards towards the centre to one outwards, until you've covered the whole ring and are back at the start of the circle again.

6　Repeat step 2 to detach the wire. Wrap the wire around five times, and leaving a tail of around 10cm, cut it. Then push the tail into the foam of the oasis.

7　Next, add your ribbon to the wreath. Make sure you leave enough length to hang it. Turn your wreath around until you find an obvious place to put it. As a guide, cut a length of ribbon and in the middle place the oasis on to it, then wrap it around on top of the foliage, tying both tails together at the top.

8　Now add your decorative touches of pine cones, cinnamon and oranges by intermittently stabbing the wire tails into the foam in either a pattern around the oasis or irregularly as you see fit.

9　Add-on options for your wreath include cutting some twigs such as willow or colourful dogwood varieties and pushing them directly into the foam at an angle. Do this all the way around the outside of the wreath. This makes the wreath bigger and more dramatic. Or add in some herbs or extra foliage such as rosemary or eucalyptus. Do this by either reattaching your wire and repeating what was initially done or stabbing the added foliage directly into the foam of the oasis.

10　Hang your wreath on your front door to welcome the coorie Christmas spirit to your home.

TEN TIPS FOR COORIE GIFT WRAPPING
Jane Adams of Author Interiors

1 We like to repurpose old newspapers found under flooring we have lifted up or in cupboards and drawers in homes we are developing or decorating, especially for our book lover friends. For friends who like something more contemporary, we like offcuts or leftover wallpaper to make an unusual and luxurious gift wrap.

2 You can get quirky with your gift tags – such as a holly leaf with your loved one's name written on it in metallic felt-tip pen. Use blackboard paint on one side of the cardboard and then write their name in chalk on it.

3 We love to bring the outside in with our Christmas decorating and wrapping, especially as Scotland has so many rich tastes, textures and scents. Posies of holly, ivy berries, and pine cones look stunning tied to presents. Dried fruits like grapefruit or orange look beautiful attached to a ribbon bow.

4 We make homemade marmalade as a Christmas tradition as a nod to the Dundee area where we live. If you have any oranges left over from making marmalade or fruit cake – cut them into slices and stick them in the oven at a low temperature so they dehydrate. For a more contemporary look, do the same with figs as they have a great texture and shape when dehydrated.

5 Try bleaching pine cones for a cool-toned vibe. Wearing gloves, bleach the cones, leaving them for less time if you prefer ashy grey or longer for white. Bleaching leaves to make leaf skeletons is another lovely addition to wrapping. You can also spray paint holly leaves and pine cones in metallic tones.

6 Think about inner wrapping as well – some tissue paper and maybe a few slices of dried blood oranges and grapefruit.

7 Consider how the gift will be received as that will affect how you dress it up. Adding a Christmas biscuit to a parcel is lovely, but not ideal if being sent in the post.

8 It's about creating scents and feelings of Christmas. Think about the texture of your wrapping, how you want it to look and how you want it to smell.

9 Set aside time for wrapping. It's all about stimulating an emotional response to Christmas. We live in a world where we are always pushed for time, so it's lovely to set aside time to do something fun and thoughtful for others. Sit in front of the fire on the floor with all your materials set out. Have a hot toddy and slice of shortbread or tablet waiting at the side as you listen to your favourite Christmas songs.

10 Darker mornings and longer, colder nights draw out from November onwards and there is less inclination to go

outside. Make use of the feeling to hibernate and make shared experiences such as the ceremony of gift wrapping as you cosy up inside during these winter months.

COORIE DECORATING FOR THE TIME POOR
Anja Baak of Great Glen Charcuterie

The run up to Christmas is always a hectic time. We are very busy getting orders out and production is at full swing, so there's not much time for relaxation.

We also have three of our children's birthdays in the month before Christmas, one at the end of November and two in the week before Christmas. We do not put any Christmas decorations up until after the birthday of our daughter Pieternel on the seventeenth of December, but often it is not until Christmas Eve that we get the house decorated.

The children decorate the Christmas tree. We have a few boxes containing lots of decorations, many handmade by them and their friends. It is lovely that they all have a story and we see them once a year. There is always a handmade angel on the top of the tree that I made many years ago.

To dress the home, I mainly use greenery from our garden such as mosses, ivy, holly and other evergreens to create decorations above the kitchen table.

The only greenery I buy each year from our local florist is eucalyptus and it appears in all decorations. I also always have a supply of florist wire that I buy online.

The decoration above our kitchen table has become a bit of a tradition now. I make one every year using just a stick from the garden, to which I attach greenery. I've stopped using foliage with needles as they tend to drop after a few days.

The fireplace display is really quickly thrown together, sometimes even on Christmas Day. I place a few candleholders on the mantle and nestle the greenery among them. I make sure I work symmetrically so there is balance at either side. I am always on the look out for silver candleholders at charity shops. Even if they are fake, the look will be uniform. I love using real wax candles in bright colours, echoing the tones of the curtains so it is a coherent look, but not so much that it feels boring.

For lighting, we have small light strings with batteries everywhere in the house to give a lovely atmosphere. I only buy soft light as I dislike the sharp blue-ish light you so often see. The battery lights are also great on outside wreaths so you don't see cables.

We are very minimalist when it comes to our outside decoration. We use a string of beautiful lights bought from Cox & Cox to decorate the courtyard area. They are often on all day during these dark winter months. In Scotland, it can make all the difference. **c**

Now playing

Deacon Blue – 'Dignity'

Coorie Continues 18

The definition of coorie may have evolved over the years but the idea of working in tandem with our homeland remains the same. If given the choice, most of us wouldn't want to swap our lives with someone richer or more talented – we just want to improve on what we already have.

What if contentment could be distilled into a few simple ideas? Well, I think it can be. Just look at the people who have evoked coorie already. Those mindful of their relationships to life's strata, others working out ways to offset their imprint on the world, and the ones allowing the stories of their past to inform the way they live now.

Coorie isn't only for Scots. Take it from me – a resident of Scotland living outside the country of my birth. I may not have started life here, but it's Scotland that's formed me. I hear that same mantra repeated time and again by people in similar circumstances.

THE PLIGHT OF THE HONEYBEE

Scotland has a knack of making newcomers feel at home, and it's not only people this rule extends to. In 2014, a colony of bees arrived in Holyrood, the Scottish parliament HQ in Edinburgh. Earlier that year the building welcomed two of its own hives, and these Buckfast Bees – which take their name from the abbey in Devon where the tonic wine is made – were chosen as the first residents because of their calm temperaments and acclimatisation to Scottish weather. The plight of the honeybee is well documented; as their natural habitat diminishes so too do their populations. But in the least obvious location – an urban square set within our wind-whipped capital – the Holyrood bees have flourished. Then, three years later, the Royal Lyceum Theatre followed suit, welcoming 70,000 bees to its rooftop as part of the Green Arts Initiative.

Now playing

King Creosote – 'No One Had It Better'

I am pleased to award the basement bars that serve cocktails featuring honey produced by Scotland's urban bees ten thousand metaphorical coorie points. They show that creative thinking can be good for the tastebuds and good for the planet.

A CALL TO ARMS

Finally, it bears repeating that an integral part of coorie is community. I started so much of my book research online, then met up with people or visited libraries, churches and museums in real life. In the same vein I'd love to hear about your coorie experiences, whether it's trying out the coorie cake or staying at one of the hideouts. I'm dying to see your pictures and I'll be checking the coorie hashtag on Instagram and Twitter regularly. The internet is where this book began, and I hope it will be where you find your next coorie idea or collaboration. Search *#theartofcoorie* for more.

You don't have to speak in a Scottish accent or have Scottish parents to feel an affinity with coorie. Scotland is too full of promise to think that people won't flow over the border and into our airports in search of something they can't find elsewhere. Equally, we may lose Scots looking for new experiences in other countries. What counts is that coorie can come with us on our travels if we adopt the right mindset. And it is always present in the land of its origin, waiting for whoever wishes to find out more. ⓒ

IMAGE CREDITS

p.v The Harris Tweed Authority
p.x James Glossop
p.1 Twenty20
p.3 Angus Bremner
p.4 Gabriella Bennett
p.5 James Glossop
p.7 James Glossop
p.8 Gabriella Bennett
p.10 Gabriella Bennett
p.10 Bute/Gordon Burniston (photo)
p.13 Mairi Helena (www.mairihelena.co.uk)
p.15 Gabriella Bennett
p.17 Mati Ventrillon
p.17 James Glossop
p.19 James Glossop
p.21 Mati Ventrillon
p.22 James Glossop
p.22 James Glossop
p.25 Gabriella Bennett
p.27 Araminta Campbell/Ciara Menzies (photo)
p.27 Hilary Grant
p.29 V&A Dundee, Photo © Ross Fraser McLean
p.30 Gabriella Bennett
p.33 James Glossop
p.35 Twenty20
p.37 James Glossop
p.37 Gabriella Bennett
p.37 Gabriella Bennett
p.38 Natural Retreats/Elly Ball (photo)
p.41 Harry Bennett
p.41 Gabriella Bennett
p.42 Eugenia Angelini/bianca_gege (instagram)
p.45 James Glossop
p.46 Gabriella Bennett
p.47 Gabriella Bennett
p.48 @tnmnttiles (twitter/instagram)
p.48 Harry Bennett
p.49 Tonje Hefte
p.51 Karl Dudman
p.51 Niall Hawley/niahaw (instagram)
p.53 Twenty20
p.54 David Gifford
p.57 Tonje Hefte
p.58 George Brown
p.61 Shutterstock
p.62 Barry Bryson
p.65 Thomas Ross
p.66 Mockford & Bonetti
p.67 Mockford & Bonetti
p.69 Gabriella Bennett
p.71 James Glossop
p.72 Andrew Ridley Photography
p.73 James Glossop
p.73 James Glossop
p.73 James Glossop
p.74 The Chippendale International School of Furniture

p.76 The Chippendale International School of Furniture
p.77 The Chippendale International School of Furniture
p.78 Ellis O'Connor
p.78 Allan Pollok Morris
p.81 Gabriella Bennett
p.82 Gabriella Bennett
p.82 Gabriella Bennett
p.83 Gabriella Bennett
p.85 James Glossop
p.86 Gabriella Bennett
p.89 Tonje Hefte
p.90 Gabriella Bennett
p.93 Gabriella Bennett
p.94 sabrinaspanke (instagram)
p.96 Jane Adams
p.98 Tonje Hefte
p.99 Tonje Hefte
p.101 Tonje Hefte
p.103 Tonje Hefte
p.105 Birgit Villand
p.106 Sarah Louise Cull
p.108 Birgit Villand
p.108 Kasia Matyjaszek
p.109 Ashton Easter
p.110 Gavin Rafferty
p.111 Gavin Rafferty
p.112 Tonje Hefte
p.113 Tonje Hefte
p.113 Twenty20
p.114 Ashton Easter
p.115 Twenty20
p.117 Twenty20
p.118 Ashton Easter
p.121 Old Bridge Inn/Chris White (photo)
p.122 Fiorella Rossi
p.123 The Pot Still/Gabriella Bennett (photo)
p.124 Scottish Horizon/Keith Fergus
p.126 Gryffe Studio
p.127 Gryffe Studio
p.128 Old Bridge Inn/Chris White (photo)
p.128 Brailey Sandlin
p.131 Emma Hargrave
p.132 Vanessa Arbuthnott
p.134 Fiona Macdonald
p.134 Fiona Macdonald
p.135 Fiona Macdonald
p.136 Alison Soye
p.137 Fiona Macdonald
p.138 Fiona Macdonald
p.140 Gabriella Bennett
p.141 Ann Fraser/Scotland's Garden Scheme
p.142 Ann Fraser/Scotland's Gardens Scheme
p.143 Emma Hargrave
p.145 Lesley McDavid/Scotland's Gardens Scheme
p.145 Lesley McDavid/Scotland's Gardens Scheme
p.146 Lesley McDavid/Scotland's Gardens Scheme

p.147 Lesley McDavid/Scotland's Gardens Scheme
p.149 Edinburgh Food Studio/Angus Behm (photo)
p.151 Old Bridge Inn/Chris White (photo)
p.151 Tonje Hefte
p.152 Karl Dudman
p.153 Harry Bennett
p.153 Harry Bennett
p.155 Gabriella Bennett
p.155 Twenty20
p.156 VSO Henderson/Gabriella Bennett (photo)
p.158 Edinburgh Food Studio/Ben Reade (photo)
p.160 Gabriella Bennett
p.163 The Harris Tweed Authority/Janet Miles (photo)
p.164 Hilary Grant
p.165 Bute/Gordon Burniston (photo)
p.166 Tonje Hefte
p.167 Bute/ Gordon Burniston (photo)
p.167 Bute/ Gordon Burniston (photo)
p.168 Tonje Hefte
p.170 Walker Slater Ltd.
p.171 The Harris Tweed Authority
p.173 The Harris Tweed Authority
p.174 The Harris Tweed Authority/Janet Miles (photo)
p.175 Mati Ventrillon
p.177 Cecilia Stamp/Caro Weiss Photography
p.178 Laura Haylock
p.179 Blair Young
p.181 Kestin Hare/Richard Gaston (photo)
p.181 Tonje Hefte
p.182 Gabriella Bennett
p.183 Hilary Grant
p.185 Cecilia Stamp/Caro Weiss Photography
p.186 Trakke Ltd.
p.189 Mati Ventrillon
p.191 Araminta Campbell/Ciara Menzies (photo)
p.192 Tonje Hefte
p.194 Object Company/Greig Jackson (photo)
p.195 Object Company/Catherine Johnston
p.195 Object Company/Catherine Johnston
p.196 Lab6/Allan Raffel (photo)
p.197 Lab6/Allan Raffel (photo)
p.199 Araminta Campbell/Ciara Menzies (photo)
p.200 Natalie J Wood/Emmi Keane/Calum Douglas
p.201 Natalie J Wood/Emmi Keane/Calum Douglas
p.202 Iona Crawford Ltd.
p.203 Iona Crawford Ltd.
p.205 Nigel Rigden (photo)/Roderick James Architects LLT (design)
p.206 Peter Buchanan
p.207 Peter Buchanan
p.208 Nigel Rigden (photo)/Roderick James Architects LLT (design)
p.210 Nigel Rigden (photo)/Roderick James Architects LLT (design)
p.211 Nigel Rigden (photo)/Roderick James Architects LLT (design)
p.212 Gabriella Bennett
p.213 Natural Retreats/Elly Ball (photo)
p.214 Natural Retreats/Hugo Petit (photo)
p.215 Natural Retreats/Hugo Petit (photo)

p.217 Anna Lamotte/Katie Goldie/Guardswell Farm
p.218 Anna Lamotte/Katie Goldie/Guardswell Farm
p.218 Anna Lamotte/Katie Goldie/Guardswell Farm
p.219 Anna Lamotte/Katie Goldie/Guardswell Farm
p.219 Anna Lamotte/Katie Goldie/Guardswell Farm
p.220 Melanie Lewis of Monachyle Mhor
p.221 Melanie Lewis of Monachyle Mhor
p.222 Melanie Lewis of Monachyle Mhor
p.222 Melanie Lewis of Monachyle Mhor
p.224 The Landmark Trust
p.225 The Landmark Trust
p.226 The Landmark Trust
p.227 The Landmark Trust
p.229 James Glossop
p.230 Hugo, North Berwick
p.232 Gabriella Bennett
p.233 Gabriella Bennett
p.234 Harry Bennett
p.235 Gabriella Bennett
p.236 Anne Hefte
p.237 Gabriella Bennett
p.238 Emma Hargrave
p.240 Tonje Hefte
p.240 Tonje Hefte
p.241 Tonje Hefte
p.243 Flora Shedden
p.243 Tonje Hefte
p.245 Tonje Hefte
p.245 Danny Walker
p.245 Tonje Hefte
p.246 Birgit Villand
p.249 AUTHOR Interiors
p.250 AUTHOR Interiors
p.251 Anja Baak
p.252 Laura Thomas Co.
p.252 Gabriella Bennett
p.252 Gabriella Bennett
p.254 Laura Thomas Co.
p.256 AUTHOR Interiors
p.256 AUTHOR Interiors
p.259 Anja Baak
p.261 Karl Dudman
p.263 Harry Bennett
p.264 Karl Dudman
p.271 James Glossop
p.275 Thomas Ross

PHOTO LOCATIONS

p.3 The Three Chimneys, Isle of Skye
p.4 Bettyhill, the Highlands
p.7 Inshriach Estate, the Highlands
p.8 Guardswell Farm, Perthshire
p.28 V&A Dundee
p.38 John o' Groats
p.41 Mangersta, Isle of Lewis
p.42 Leakey's, Inverness
p.51 Glasgow city centre
p.58 Aberdour, Fife
p.64 Tolsta Chaolais, Isle of Lewis
p.68 Arivruaich, Isle of Lewis
p.70 Inshriach Estate, the Highlands
p.78 Sweeney's Bothy, Isle of Eigg
p.84 Edinburgh skyline
p.89 The Shore, Leith
p.94 Ashton Lane, Glasgow
p.104 The West Highland Way
p.106 Loch Maree, Wester Ross
p.108 The West Highland Way
p.108 Isle of Seil
p.109 Ardnamurchan Point, the Highlands
p.110 Glen Docherty, Wester Ross
p.111 Bealach na Bà, Wester Ross
p.114 Loch an Dubh-Lochain
p.124 Sligachan, Isle of Skye
p.148 Edinburgh Food Studio
p.168 Upper Bow, Edinburgh
p.178 South Queensferry Steps Mural
p.182 Earl's Palace, Birsay, Orkney
p.207 Lammermuir Hills, the Borders
p.230 North Berwick
p.234 Scolpaig Tower, North Uist
p.260 Mallaig
p.263 Arivruaich, Isle of Lewis
p.274 Valtos beaches, Isle of Lewis

PROP CREDITS

FURTHER READING

Allan, Geoff, *The Scottish Bothy Bible* (Wild Things Publishing Ltd, 2017)

Barber, E.J.W., *Prehistoric Textiles: The Development Of Cloth In The Neolithic And Bronze Ages With Special Reference To The Aegean* (Princeton University Press, 1992)

Boswell, James, *The Journal of a Tour to the Hebrides* (Penguin Classics, 1984)

Faber, Michel, *Under the Skin* (Canongate Books, 2017)

McGuire, Ian, *The North Water* (Scribner UK, 2016)

Grant, Kimberley; Gaston, Richard; Cooper, David, *Wild Guide Scotland: Hidden Places, Great Adventures and the Good Life* (Wild Things Publishing Ltd, 2017)

Liptrot, Amy, *The Outrun* (Canongate Books, 2016)

Spark, Muriel, *The Prime of Miss Jean Brodie* (Macmillan, 1961)

Smith, Ali, *Girl Meets Boy* (Canongate Books, 2007)

Tandoh, Ruby, *Eat Up! Food, Appetite and Eating What You Want* (Serpent's Tail, 2018)

ACKNOWLEDGEMENTS

Thank you to Walter Micklethwait, who let us shoot some of *The Art of Coorie*'s photography on his estate.

Special shout out to Lizzy Westman and her lifesaving apricot jam toast.

To Natasha Radmehr, for her impeccable taste, and to James Glossop, for taking pictures that looked better than I could have ever imagined.

To Helen Bashforth, for her research on coorie textiles.

To Jennie Patterson, the high priestess of contacts, for hooking me up with people in the biz.

To Brenda Anderson at Tasting Scotland for her guidance on smoking food, and to Scott Smith at Norn for keeping me right with pine needles.

To *The Times*, for letting me go part time while I wrote this book.

To all at Black & White for enabling me to work on the project of my dreams. And Craig Gallacher, who understood perfectly what I was hoping to create in designing the book.

To all at Scotland's Gardens, especially Terrill Dobson and Imogen McCaw, for finding me some incredible green-fingered people.

To Martin Schauss, life coach, scrambled egg extraordinaire, best one.

To all those whose coorie thoughts and memories I have quoted on pages 39, 40, 70, 91, 128, 193 and 216.

To all the makers, designers, business owners, chefs, bar tenders, and gardeners who gave their time and wisdom so graciously. *The Art of Coorie* wouldn't exist without you.

MY COORIE PROJECTS

GABRIELLA BENNETT is a journalist based in Glasgow. She writes for *The Times* about Scottish interiors, property and shopping habits. Researching *The Art of Coorie* she travelled the length and breadth of Scotland speaking to people whose love of coorie is shown in their homes, creativity and approach to a life lived well. Best of all, it gave her the chance to explore the Scottish landscape by swimming in its lochs and seas. *The Art of Coorie* is Gabriella's first book. You can find her at gabriellabennett.com and @palebackwriter. ℮